The One
Page CV

PEARSON

At Pearson, we believe in learning – all kinds of learning for all kinds of people. Whether it's at home, in the classroom or in the workplace, learning is the key to improving our life chances.

That's why we're working with leading authors to bring you the latest thinking and the best practices, so you can get better at the things that are important to you. You can learn on the page or on the move, and with content that's always crafted to help you understand quickly and apply what you've learned.

If you want to upgrade your personal skills or accelerate your career, become a more effective leader or more powerful communicator, discover new opportunities or simply find more inspiration, we can help you make progress in your work and life.

Pearson is the world's leading learning company. Our portfolio includes the Financial Times, Penguin, Dorling Kindersley, and our educational business, Pearson International.

Every day our work helps learning flourish, and wherever learning flourishes, so do people.

To learn more please visit us at: **www.pearson.com/uk**

The One Page CV

Paul Hichens

PEARSON

Harlow, England • London • New York • Boston • San Francisco • Toronto • Sydney
Auckland • Singapore • Hong Kong • Tokyo • Seoul • Taipei • New Delhi
Cape Town • São Paulo • Mexico City • Madrid • Amsterdam • Munich • Paris • Milan

PEARSON EDUCATION LIMITED
Edinburgh Gate
Harlow CM20 2JE
United Kingdom
Tel: +44 (0)1279 623623
Web: www.pearson.com/uk

First published 2013 (print and electronic)

© Pearson Education Limited (print and electronic)

The right of Paul Hichens to be identified as author of this work has been asserted by him in accordance with the Copyright, Designs and Patents Act 1988.

Pearson Education is not responsible for the content of third-party internet sites.

ISBN: 978-1-292-00147-0 (print)
        978-1-292-00148-7 (PDF)
        978-1-292-00149-4 (ePub)
        978-1-292-00808-0 (eText)

British Library Cataloguing-in-Publication Data
A catalogue record for the print edition is available from the British Library

Library of Congress Cataloging-in-Publication Data
Hichens, Paul.
  The one page CV / Paul Hichens.
     pages cm
  Includes bibliographical references and index.
  ISBN 978-1-292-00147-0 (print) -- ISBN 978-1-292-00148-7 (PDF) -- ISBN 978-1-292-00149-4
  (ePub) -- ISBN 978-1-292-00808-0 (eText)
  1. Résumés (Employment) 2. Job hunting. I. Title.
  HF5383.H496 0013
  650.14'2--dc23
                          2013033064

10 9 8 7 6 5 4 3 2 1
17 16 15 14 13

Illustrations by Ken Pyne
Cover design by Kit Foster

Print edition typeset in10.25/14 pt Frutiger LT Pro by 30
Print edition printed and bound in Great Britain by Henry Ling Ltd, at the Dorest Press, Dorchester, Dorset

NOTE THAT ANY PAGE CROSS REFERENCES REFER TO THE PRINT EDITION

For Mary and Allan, mam and dad.

Luckily you don't need a CV when you are retired, but if I wrote one for you it'd show the world that you are wonderful people, loving parents and fantastic, doting grandparents.

I know just a few words on a page will never repay even a fraction of everything you have given me, but if anything I'm a trier …

Contents

5 CV writing myths 81

About the author:
a mini CV of sorts …

Paul Hichens is one of the UK's foremost CV writers. In addition to advising on CVs in public and on the BBC, Paul is very much in demand for his work and has had a long and constant waiting list for many years now.

Clients from all walks of life come to him on a regular basis from every corner of the globe, many by personal recommendation.

Over the years Paul has not only helped a great many people into better jobs, but has also long been an incisive and fruitful source of career advice to job seekers at all levels and across all sectors.

Bilingual and with a Master's degree, Paul's passion is creative writing. He is also an accomplished musician, singer and songwriter.

Acknowledgements

It never ceases to surprise me that people write their own DIY CV and apply for (and frequently miss out on) good jobs without at the very least getting a free second opinion from a professional.

As you will quickly surmise, I am a professional writer, and in addition to people in typical everyday jobs, my clients include other writers and people in related professions such as recruiters, HR executives, journalists, editors, heads of communication etc. In fact, I am a source of help for a whole host of people who you wouldn't think needed it.

With that in mind it may well surprise you all the more to hear that I too sought help from someone when preparing this book, and I am extremely grateful indeed to Sylvia Jobar for her invaluable advice and insightful recommendations. Sylvia is wonderfully creative and a highly talented writer in her own right, and her help stretched far beyond mere editing.

I'm also very grateful to Eloise Cook not only for her editorial expertise, but also for her support, encouragement and enthusiasm. Publishers are often inundated with submissions, and picking out the gems can be akin to finding if not a needle in a haystack, then at least a bookmark in a library. I am indebted to Eloise for her persistence and rummaging prowess. I was always quite good at hide-and-seek as a child, but was becoming somewhat dismayed and frustrated that this chameleon characteristic seemed to be continuing into adulthood. For once I'm glad that someone finally found me – and that someone was Eloise.

I would also like to take this opportunity to thank the exceptionally talented people I have worked with over the years at CV Succeed. Kathie, Sylvia (again), Rachel, Norman and Steph I have no doubt whatsoever that you are the best CV writers in the world bar none, and it is an absolute privilege to work with you. If I ever wanted help with my own CV I wouldn't dream of going to anyone else. Of course, there is more to helping people than just writing; and Peter Green has always been a reliable, trustworthy and quite simply brilliant customer services manager, while in the background Jai, Niki and the girls have consistently ensured that the techie things tick, and the admin cogs tock and turn like clockwork.

Last but no means least, I'd like to thank all the many customers we have helped over the years – a bit of an unusual acknowledegment for the genre granted, but most CV book authors don't actually write CVs for a living, and those specialists who do don't seem to have a book in them – how's that for irony?

I've always encouraged clients to provide feedback (good or bad), and while 99.99 per cent of comments have been extremely complimentary, I have also found the other 0.01 per cent of feedback useful too since it has helped me examine and analyse my CV methodology more than I would have done otherwise. Moreover, the very act of explaining the advantages of doing things a certain way has proved to be very beneficial. First, it served to stimulate my already inquisitive snout into rooting round a whole range of CV-related issues all the more – and delving even deeper into the subject. Secondly, the more I strove to find answers to questions and solutions to problems the more I came to realise that I was amassing some sizeable, quality material for a great book.

Clients everywhere, give yourself a huge pat on the back; you have not only given me a great deal of job satisfaction over the years, but unbeknown to you, you've even helped write this book.

Whoops – can we just forget I said that last bit? The royalty cheques start coming in soon!

The best CV you'll ever write

Calling all non-parrots

This book will help you like no other in the genre. In fact, there is no other like this available. It is a refreshingly new and unique career liberation tool – helping you write just what it says on the tin – a winning one-page CV. Significantly, the book neither encourages nor teaches you to copy CVs parrot-fashion. If that is what you are looking for, and you really do want just to blend in with the crowd, then pretty much all other CV books are tailor-made for that purpose.

'But what if I want to stand out?'

Ah, if you really *do* want to stand out from the crowd, then the good news is that this book is the spark, fuse and dynamite that can quite literally blast your career into a dramatic new stratosphere.

Yes, the methods and lessons you will learn are new, radical and different, but they have been developed by arguably the UK's leading CV visionary, and significantly they work, and work far more successfully than those of typical CV books.

Talking of typical advice ...

There are many rungs on the career ladder and possibilities abound for you to climb all the way up to your target job – and especially if you go about things the right way. And there is no doubt that a top quality CV can help you travel further and faster up the career ladder than an average or even a good CV.

Pretty much everyone has the potential to improve their career prospects, but many people just do not know how to maximise their potential – it is far easier said than done after all. Little wonder then that many job seekers seek CV advice from the likes of family and colleagues. This is all perfectly natural, but there is a lot more to CV writing than meets the eye and a lot of well-meaning advice from friends does more harm than good. And it's not only laypeople who can sometimes harm your career prospects: some of the things you might read in other books, or hear from the likes of Job Centre advisers or certain recruitment companies can see you stagnate indefinitely on that same old career rung, rather than move up to the job that you really want. Indeed, a surprising amount of advice from so-called experts is potentially highly counterproductive.

Among other things, this book will help you look at typical CV advice more objectively and identify the good from the bad and the valid from the unsound.

Why a one-page CV?

Well, you said you wanted to stand out didn't you? And nothing stands out more than a quality one-page CV – which explains why they are becoming increasingly popular, not only with people in the know such as HR executives, marketing experts and heads of communications, but with job seekers at all levels and in all sectors.

And it's not just about standing out either. Yes, it certainly helps if you can attract the employer's attention, but beyond that you still need a clear, focused, high-impact sales message. But get this – well-written one-page CVs can be (and often are) far more effective at selling than their longer counterparts.

'But I'll never fit everything on just one page' I hear you cry. And if you followed conventional CV advice you probably wouldn't – but this is no normal book, and the CV you create will be anything but average.

You may think that dramatically shortening a CV without adversely affecting its effectiveness is impossible. However, you would be surprised. It's my experience that many people have between 20 and 50 per cent (or more) of superfluous information on their CV. So, as surprising as this may sound, it is highly likely that you do too. If so, don't worry – this book will show you not only how to fix that issue, but also how to make your CV more powerful into the bargain.

The best CV in the world

'Is there such a thing?'

Yes – but not in a form that you know. Indeed, as you will discover, the best CV in the world is a complex, multifaceted chameleon.

An enigmatic beast it may be, but if you do manage to corner, tame and master it, then it could be the best thing that ever happened to your career.

Lessons you will learn

... in short how to write by far and away your best-ever CV. One that is more relevant, more focused, better optimised and sells you infinitely better to employers than you would create by copying examples or following the advice given in other books ...

As mentioned, the purpose of this book is to help you write a winning CV, one which can truly help propel you up the career ladder. You are unlikely to achieve this with a typical CV, using run-of-the-mill methods and copying well-worn examples which end up wearily doing the rounds of the job circuit.

If you are truly serious about scaling the career ladder then you actually need the *best possible CV*; even a good quality CV may not suffice. I reiterate, you need the *best possible CV* – which is individually crafted for you, your own circumstances and which is meticulously optimised for your own target job.

This book teaches you just that and a whole lot more besides. It should help you not only write the best CV you have ever written, but in addition to that it will show you how to 'sell' rather than 'tell' and also how to become a far better communicator in general – not bad traits to have – and ones which you can use to your advantage time and again to help propel you up the career ladder.

Admittedly, this all sounds daunting, and perhaps even impossible. But as you will learn, it is within your reach right now.

Read on with open eyes, ears and mind.

1

CV overview

CV writing in perspective

All CVs are equal, but some are more equal than others. PAUL HICHENS

The vast majority of people think CV writing is easy. In fact, the belief that it is possible to 'knock up a CV in a couple of hours' is not uncommon. Traditionally most people write CVs themselves and, having examined thousands of DIY CVs over the years, I know that many people actually spend less than two or three hours on their CV.

This would be all well and good if it were a level playing field, and everyone played by the same two- or three-hour rule. However, some people are cannier than others, and while you might spend no more than three hours working on your CV, some of your competitors will spend eight hours working solidly on theirs.

Of course, time is not the all-important factor here: quality is. Nevertheless, the above example should at least serve to show that some people take their CV more seriously than others. Significantly, it is those people who take their CV more seriously who tend to make faster and greater strides up the career ladder. You could be the best in the world in your particular field, but if you skimp on thought, time, fine detail and quality when writing your CV then you will probably have less chance of getting a job than someone who is only half as good but whose CV is better.

Great CVs open doors, whilst poor (or even good) CVs close them.

Rome wasn't built in a day. But I wasn't on that particular job. BRIAN CLOUGH

SO HOW LONG SHOULD YOU TAKE WRITING YOUR CV?

The answer to this is pretty simple on the surface: *as long as it takes to get it right*. But that is rather like asking how long is a piece of string.

Another way of putting it is to say it should take as long as necessary to satisfy yourself (or better still an employer) that your CV is slick, error-free, professional-looking and the ideal length. Not only that, but it should be well-balanced, portray you over and above your competitors as an achiever, and sell your skills in a sharp, punchy and legible manner. It should bring out your relevant personal traits as well as your professional skills and competencies. Your CV should address the job in question and be tuned in to what the employer is looking for. It needs to be pitched at the right level, realistically, logically and in the right tone. Its message should be focused, strong and powerful. Most importantly, it should entice the employer to read it all the way to the end with ever-increasing interest, not give up after just 6 seconds. And if you think that is an exaggeration then think again. Employers are very busy people, they receive heaps of applications, and if yours doesn't hit the spot almost instantaneously then your CV is likely to find itself looking gloomily down from the top of the rejects mountain, rather than sitting smug and pretty, in pride of place on the short list.

If you are one of the many who had previously thought that CV writing was easy, and you are also guilty of just spending two or three hours to write your own CV then perhaps the above paragraph will give you some food for thought. Yes, admittedly any Tom, Dick or Harry can write a CV *of sorts* in a couple of hours. However, nothing of true value in life comes easy, and if you are serious about landing the job of your dreams then you are unlikely to do it with an average DIY CV, especially when you will almost certainly be competing against people who are prepared to do whatever it takes to submit the best possible application. This not only includes people who are prepared to spend many hours burning the midnight oil working on their CV, but it also includes job seekers who are willing to pay a skilled professional to do the writing for them.

Not everyone has the resources or inclination to engage a professional writer, and if you fall into this category then the following advice should help you improve your own CV dramatically. As with pretty much everything else in this book, it is not all typical advice. While some traditional advice is useful, I believe that a lot of it is counterproductive. For me, typical advice on the whole is too inflexible and paints the same fantasy pictures with a multi-purpose brush. Consequently, the end results often bear more bitter and less bountiful fruit than initially promised.

With that in mind, in addition to identifying the pitfalls of typical advice (and showing you better alternatives), this book also should give you ample food for thought and plenty of ammunition for the next time a lesser recruiter* with no real CV knowledge or understanding tries to bamboozle you with their weird brand of curriculum vitae fables, junk and jargon.

---

* Please note that some people confuse recruiters with employers. However, there is an important and significant distinction. Employers and HR executives are the real decision makers, and ultimately decide whether or not you get the job. Recruiters on the other hand do not have the same say/influence. Indeed, for the most part they are effectively just go-betweens or middlemen. As such they should not be confused with *real* employers. Make no mistake, the most important person you need to impress with your CV is not the go-between recruiter, but the real employer. You'll be glad to hear that this book has been specifically designed to help you impress employers – and like never before!

2

CV templates, CV examples and sheep

As mentioned, a lot of typical CV advice is counterproductive. To help you spot potential dangers I have incorporated a traffic light signalling system throughout this book; with green (the bottom light) as *safe*, amber (the middle light) for *proceed with caution*, and red (the top light) at the more perilous end of the scale. Templates come under red! As this book is in greyscale you may have to use your imagination a tad.

He's going for the pink, and for those of you with black-and-white [TV] sets, the yellow is behind the blue. TED LOWE, SNOOKER COMMENTATOR

 ... among other things that templates are not all that they seem. This section can help you skip past the nasty potential falls that catch out so many job seekers ...

Templates precursor

Reason is the wise man's guide, example the fool's.
WELSH PROVERB

Personally, I think typical CV advice lacks imagination, lucidity, flexibility and honesty. People are shepherded like lost sheep down the same well-trodden route, lured by the impossible one-serves-all promise of *follow me to your ideal job*.

If someone told you to wear the same outfit as everyone else at interview you would think it was a rather odd way of trying to get yourself noticed. But this is precisely what some CV advice does. And it is also one reason why I'm not a big fan of CV templates and sample CVs. Besides the fact that they draw people down the same path (whether it is the right path or not), they also have the inevitable but undesirable effect of stifling one's own initiative, intuition and creativity. CV templates and samples create a tendency to draw the job seeker into following the example given, rather than encouraging them to use their own intelligence and common sense to come up with something which is not only more personalised, original and suitable, but also far better. Little wonder so many employers get bored with the same old bog-standard CVs.

As a bit of an aside: I was asked, along with some others, by someone who works with CVs what I thought of an American résumé-writing book he had bought. (If you're unfamiliar with the term résumé, it is effectively the US equivalent of CV.) Apparently it is a very popular book and has sold a great many copies. He opened it at a random page showing a sample résumé and asked for opinions. In turn, everyone examined the page studiously without saying a word. When it came to my turn, however, I just burst out laughing. The others looked puzzled, so I asked them what they thought of it. They replied that it looked okay to them. I then asked them what the first paragraph meant. This stumped them. It was so long-winded and full of jargon that none of them had any idea what it actually meant. They couldn't say what message the author was trying to relay, presumably because there wasn't really a message at all. Or certainly not a clear and unambiguous one.

I think people sometimes see something written in long-winded, convoluted jargon, but, because it is in print and on the surface seems intellectual, they fight their natural impulse of *this is utter gibberish* and instead convince themselves that the text must be right. Consequently, the tendency is for the reader to conform to the text, and not the other way around.

I do not doubt that there will be a great many people around the world copying this sample résumé to the letter every single day. There must be thousands doing the rounds by now and I suspect that every day there will be a great many employers around the world who read this résumé, scratch their head, and wonder what the hell the candidate is talking about.

The same applies to a great many other sample CVs and cover letters. When considering the use of sample CVs and templates you should ask yourself:

- Do I really want to write the same CV as everyone else?

- Will the sample get an employer to sit up and take notice of me?

- Does it really represent me and what I, personally, can offer?

- Is the sample actually any good anyway?

If the answer to any of the above is 'no' then you may wish to ask yourself another question:

- Do I want an original CV which emphasises my own positives, my own traits, skills and expertise, and which is written with the job and the employer in mind?

Obviously it is up to you whether or not this is something you would like, but if it were me then I most certainly would want such a CV as opposed to a typical sample CV.

CV templates and examples

Good advice is something a man gives when he is too old to set a bad example.
FRANCOIS DE LA ROCHEFOUCAULD

When most people buy a CV book the first thing they usually look for are the templates and examples. After this, the next step is usually to dive in headfirst and eagerly start copying one of the samples, sporting a smug '*job done*' grin as they tap away at their keyboard.

For the uninitiated, *templates* are effectively CV skeletons that you can use as a base for your CV. These are useful if you want something quick that looks good. CV *examples*, on the other hand, don't necessarily look the part, but they include content that is relevant and (sometimes) written well, and can give you ideas for the content of your own CV.

If you have read the contents list for the rest of this book you will not be surprised to learn that the templates/examples section here is somewhat different from the norm. So, rather than blindly extolling the virtues of templates then shooing you all away with a piece of tracing paper each, I will be doing something rather unusual: namely, alerting you to the dangers of copying them. Indeed, such are the dangers of copying templates that there is even a danger associated with copying the best ones. Of course, you do need a point of reference, so I will lead you in the direction of the format I have found to be the best of them all. Significantly, even though it is a great format, and is tried and tested in the job market, there are still some associated dangers with copying it. Whatever templates you are contemplating using, this chapter should alert you to the potential risks, and help prevent them from backfiring in your face.

Good quality CV examples are actually few and far between. And I strongly suspect that many of the example CVs doing the rounds on the internet have been written (or more likely plagiarised and tweaked) by web designers and web copywriters rather than real CV writers or anyone with genuine CV experience. Nevertheless, this still doesn't stop prospective job hunters from blindly copying them in their thousands.

That said, some good examples do exist, and especially specifically targeted CV examples that have been written by real CV writers. You can expect to pay for the better quality CV examples but, unlike the poor quality free ones, at least with the more impressive examples you can take out the best bits and adapt them for your own needs.

At the same time you need to keep everything in perspective, and realise that, no matter what, you still need to use your own intelligence and creativity rather than simply put all your faith in a document which by its very nature is general, impersonal and somewhat detached from you, your needs, your circumstances and your own individual desires.

You may think I'm joking, but I can assure you that if I could I would have a big flashing brightly coloured animated image here saying:

Templates and examples beware!

However, I don't and it isn't, so you are going to have to remember it yourselves. Saying that, to help you do so, I will be providing evidence to demonstrate why it pays to beware of CV templates and examples.

The long and short of er ... CV length among other things

Learn the fundamentals of the game and stick to them. Band-Aid remedies never last. JACK NICKLAUS

... among other things, how to spot good from bad as well as some important CV fundamentals that are frequently overlooked ...

As I'm sure you are well aware, templates come in a variety of shapes, sizes and formats, ranging from long to short, good to bad, old-school to contemporary, conventional to weird, and common to all too common. There are probably hundreds of different CV templates, and depending upon who you listen to their format will be better than everyone else's. Obviously, with so many different templates doing the rounds this is quite some claim. However, there is no shortage of so-called experts and CV book authors telling you and all and sundry that their particular format is without a shadow of a doubt the best one ever made, and that if you copy their formula you will be sitting behind a new desk smoking a big cigar within a week.

For those of you who haven't already excitedly rushed out of the door, lighter in hand, I'm happy to elaborate:

Over the years I have examined a great many CV formats/templates, and have not only tried them out, but have also gauged opinions from employers, HR executives, recruiters and designers. Almost inevitably, many of these opinions differ, although there is a general consensus on most of the key issues. For example, it is commonly recognised that the best CV formats are presentable, legible, a good length, well structured and evoke excellent first impressions. It is generally accepted that the best CVs look something like a well-balanced framed picture, as shown overleaf. If you look closely, you will see that this CV uses single-line bullet points rather than multi-line paragraphs, plus decent margins all the way around and a good general balance. Talking of balance, it is better to have CVs which fill all of their pages, rather than CVs consisting of, for example, just one and a bit pages.

In addition to this, there are other more intangible factors to weigh up when considering CV templates. For example, you may have a CV which is presentable, well structured and a good length, but if the layout is such that it restricts the word count so that you can't say everything you need to say within the optimum length then there is clearly a problem. Alarmingly, numerous highly presentable and seemingly attractive templates fall into this category.

Mike Hewitt

♦ 9 Park Road, London, SW1 3FP ♦ 0207 946 0379 ♦ mike.hewitt76@yahoo.com

PERSONAL PROFILE

The top of your CV is where your personal profile usually goes. It is also best to keep it concise and relevant. You will learn more about profiles later in this book.

CAREER & ACHIEVEMENTS TO DATE

Senior Account Manager   2005–date
EMC Corporation, London

KEY ACHIEVEMENTS
♦ Conventionally, your career or work experience section usually comes next
♦ Although sometimes it pays to include it further down your CV
♦ You will learn more about writing flexibly with the employer in mind later in this book
♦ Your career section is often pivotal and can make or break your job application
♦ See how neat and presentable it looks if you use well-spaced bullet points
♦ It's better if you use single-line bullets like this, rather than paragraphs/multiple lines
♦ Single-line bullets improves legibility and helps get your message across more effectively
♦ Of course it isn't easy to refine your achievements down to neat, proactive statements
♦ But it is possible if you know how, and this book will help you write more succinctly
♦ Yes, you still need to sell yourself, but we'll learn more about writing powerfully later
♦ In fact we will learn a whole lot more than just the usual CV basics in this book
♦ You need to take a more holistic approach if you want to create a real top-quality CV
♦ And master more key CV aspects than many (including other CV book authors) knew existed
♦ But be patient my friend, we will get there in good time, and your CV will improve *dramatically*

QUALIFICATIONS

MBA (Oxford University)   2004
BSc in Business Studies (London University)   1998

SKILLS & KEY COMPETENCIES

♦ Here is where you can add skills   ♦ You will learn more about skills
♦ And key competencies   ♦ And how to sell yourself powerfully
♦ Not just any old skills or competencies ♦ Read on with open mind ...
♦ Even skills sections need method   ♦ You'll be glad you did

INTERESTS & REFERENCES

Interests: Photography, Opera and Cycling | References Available on Request

In the course of my research and experiments I have found that while some formats score well on, for instance, presentation, they perhaps fall down on other areas such as structure or their ability to get your sales message across properly. Indeed, I have found that most formats are flawed in one way or another.

As it happens, I do have a preferred format of sorts. As you can imagine, it isn't one I hit upon by chance, but is one which firstly scored very highly in my experiments, and which I then subsequently refined. I will introduce you to this format later in this chapter, but one thing I will say about it at this stage is that even though it is the best format I have found, I still don't treat it as a cast-iron formula which I use in exactly the same way each and every time. On the contrary, even though this format scores highly on just about every front, I still take a flexible approach with it, and amend it depending upon the circumstances (which is why I say it is my preferred format *of sorts*).

Significantly, even though this particular format came top in my experiments, and it is extremely popular, I would still be open to the possibility of changing it for another format if someone came up with one which was more effective. As it happens, it is a habit of mine to look at any new CV format I come across. So far I haven't seen one which I think would work better than my preferred format, but you just never know; which is why I keep an open mind on the subject.

Anyway, without further ado let's have a look at an example.

The following was sent to me by someone who said they had rewritten their CV following the instructions on a template they liked. The person in question had applied for jobs unsuccessfully with it and wanted to know my opinion. I have included the CV, but to conceal the individual's identity I have changed his name and address as well as some dates and job details. For the purposes of this book I have also shortened the CV considerably.

Looking at the CV format as a whole, it is quite common and probably hundreds if not thousands of people have their CV in exactly this format. What about you? Have a look at your CV now and see how

Mark Chapman

1 Church Street
Broomhill
Sheffield
South Yorkshire
S13 3BB
Home Tel No: 0113 496 0133
Mobile: 07700 903246
Email: MC78@hotmail.com
Nationality: British

PERSONAL STATEMENT

An experienced negotiator and project manager who consistently delivers improvements in the construction industry.

I'm a team player, who sets the standard through my enthusiasm, dedication and hard work.

I have liaised with developers and clients and have established new clients and retained the existing ones.

I'm looking forward to working for a leading construction company.

EDUCATION

Year	Institute	Location
2000	Surrey University	**Guildford**

Qualification
BSc Construction Management

Year	Institute	Location
1996	King Henry's School	**York**

Qualification
eight GCSEs and three A-levels

TECHNICAL SKILLS

- MS Access   Basic
- PowerPoint   Basic
- Microsoft Word   Intermediate

WORK EXPERIENCE

Date 2004–present	Name of Company	Location
	ABC Ltd	**Sheffield**

Responsibilities
- Liaised with developers and clients
- Established new clients and retained the existing ones
- Negotiated rebates and agreements with new developers

Date 2001–2004	Name of Company	Location
	DEG Ltd	**Sheffield**

Responsibilities
- Worked on a variety of construction projects
- Led a team of 8 on a new build

INTERESTS

- Watching sport
- Golf

REFERENCES

Referees available on request.

it compares. Does it have many similarities? Do you think your CV would be improved if it looked like the above template?

- Yes?
- No?

Sometimes not everything is as it appears. So before you rush to the stationery cupboard to dig out your tracing paper and start copying, let us first examine the template in greater detail.

The first section is shown here.

Mark Chapman

1 Church Street
Broomhill
Sheffield
South Yorkshire
S13 3BB
Home Tel No: 0113 496 0133
Mobile: 07700 903246
Email: MC78@hotmail.com
Nationality: British

It is quite a common opening, and there are thousands if not millions of CVs worldwide with an opening along these lines. What about your CV? Is it similar? And what do you think?

- Good?
- Bad?
- Average?
- Insignificant?

For my part, there are two things which strike me about this. First, it takes up an awful lot of vertical space (far too much space), but perhaps of even more significance is the fact that the name and address are the most prominent things on the whole CV. This is not only unnecessary, but it is also going to do very little when it comes to the important matter of letting the employer know quickly and in no uncertain terms what your specialism is. Yes, with this format the employer will quickly know that you live in a particular street in Sheffield. Unfortunately, however, this is hardly going to matter because unless you impress the employer enough with your CV in the first place you are unlikely to receive a letter through the post inviting you to interview anyway.

The second section is shown next.

PERSONAL STATEMENT

An experienced negotiator and project manager who consistently delivers improvements in the construction industry.
I'm a team player, who sets the standard through my enthusiasm, dedication and hard work.
I have liaised with developers and clients and have established new clients and retained the existing ones.
I'm looking forward to working for a leading construction company.

Adding a personal statement or a profile is conventional and is something which I too advocate. Before reading on, compare it with yours and just decide whether or not you think this (and yours) is a good profile.

For me, this one isn't particularly powerful. I asked the candidate what his rationale was for the profile, and his response was that the advice given on the template was to list your achievements and your career objectives. I find this rather strange. There is no value in repeating work achievements. The best place for work achievements are in the work achievements section. Similarly, as mentioned elsewhere in this book, there is little value in adding career objectives in your profile either.

The third section is next to be considered.

EDUCATION

Year	Institute	Location
2000	Surrey University	**Guildford**
	Qualification	
	BSc Construction Management	
Year	Institute	Location
1996	King Henry's School	**York**
	Qualification	
	eight GCSEs and three A-levels	

I have several issues with this. First, the header *education* isn't particularly proactive and would be better replaced by the more positive term *qualifications*. Secondly, the placement of this section is more in line with a typical student CV, not a professional one. Thirdly, the template wording led the candidate down the false path of thinking that candidates are obliged to include all their qualifications in their CV. They are not, and sometimes (as discussed elsewhere) it can be counterproductive. This reiterates an important concept which I have already touched upon: namely, that the best CVs are written flexibly, and if you follow a rigid path (which many people following a template do) it can be (and often is) counterproductive.

In this instance the candidate has wasted vertical space (space which could be far better used selling his skills) mentioning qualifications which are pretty much irrelevant and are superseded by a relevant degree anyway. I asked the candidate why he included them, and his response was that there were two lines for education on the template and he just filled in the gaps. Proof in itself that if you follow templates without really thinking it could be detrimental to your job prospects.

On to the next section.

TECHNICAL SKILLS	
▪ MS Access	Basic
▪ PowerPoint	Basic
▪ Microsoft Word	Intermediate

Again, one of the main problems I have with this is that the template has given the candidate the false impression that he has to include technical skills. This just isn't so; it really depends on the job you are going for and what the employer is looking for. Significantly, even if technical skills are required then just having a few unsubstantiated bullet points near the top of your CV isn't really going to wow the employer. The way to do that is through concrete, impressive, fully backed-up work achievements. If anything, the information here is detrimental, because quite clearly the candidate doesn't have good IT skills, and the inclusion of this section near the top of his CV is just drawing unnecessary attention to this unfortunate fact.

We are already halfway down the CV and there has been no real opportunity to highlight effectively the candidate's expertise and specialism. So far the CV has been mainly concerned with comparatively trivial things like letting the employer know where the candidate lives, what GCSEs he possesses and how much MS Access experience he has. I can't vouch for all employers, but I strongly suspect that many would have given up the ghost by this stage. Employers are busy people and don't have the time to wade more than halfway through a CV before they come to anything of note.

Now we come onto the next section.

WORK EXPERIENCE

Date 2004–present   Name of Company   Location
                                  ABC Ltd   **Sheffield**

Responsibilities
- Liaised with developers and clients
- Established new clients and retained the existing ones
- Negotiated rebates and agreements with new developers

Date 2001–2004   Name of Company   Location
                                  DEG Ltd   **Sheffield**

Responsibilities
- Worked on a variety of construction projects
- Led a team of 8 on a new build

At last! Something the employer can possibly get their teeth into (if he or she manages to hang around this long to find out – remember that sometimes just 6 seconds is all you get to make the right impression). The section also includes single-line bullet points, which is a good idea, and an excellent way of presenting work achievements.

Saying that, the section still leaves a lot to be desired. For starters, the term *work experience* is quite passive. Something along the lines of *career and achievements to date* would be more proactive. Similarly, the term *responsibilities* is somewhat passive, and isn't as strong as the term *achievements*. You want to come across as an achiever after all.

While I have seen better work experience sections, at least this one incorporates the fundamentals. That said, just going by the terminology and the way it is set out, I strongly suspect that many people who copied this template ended up with a work experience section along the lines of *I did this* and *I did that* rather than *I did this to achieve that and it had this really positive outcome*. This is highly significant, because as we will later learn, the best CVs *sell* rather than *tell*, and powerful achievements are part and parcel of that.

What about your CV?

- Does it do a good job of selling you powerfully and instantaneously?
- Are you making the most of the very limited space available?

If not then don't worry, we'll cover all that later – all in good time.

All in all, this template looks quite presentable, arguably better than most, and I can see why some people would be tempted to use it. However, as illustrated, just following templates willy-nilly is often counterproductive. And this template is no exception to the rule.

Template sources

Few things are harder to put up with than the annoyance of a good example. PUDDN'HEAD WILSON (MARK TWAIN)

BIG FLASHING LIGHT!

Okay, so there isn't really a big flashing light here, but the heading serves a purpose, and in this case it is to warn you about something else: namely, the fact that just because templates and examples come from a respected source it doesn't necessarily mean they are any good.

Below is the link to a CV sample, which at the time of writing was recommended by the government website Directgov: **http://www. direct.gov.uk/prod_consum_dg/groups/dg_digitalassets/@dg/@en/ @employ/documents/digitalasset/dg_173861.pdf**

At the time of writing they also listed a sample cover letter here: **http://www.direct.gov.uk/en/Employment/Jobseekers/Helpapplyingforajob/DG_173634**

It's up to you whether or not you take a look. For my part, let's just say that the sample cover letter isn't one I would personally use, and the CV wasn't one of the templates that made my short list. (That's me being rather tactful. I'll let you read between the lines to guess what I really think of them. Suffice to say that, as mentioned, an official source doesn't mean to say it is any good – sometimes it's the advisers rather than the job seekers who are in greater need of counsel.) Please note that these links were live at the time of publication. I dare say this could possibly change at some point if one of my readers gives them a tip-off!

GREEN LIGHT SETTING GOOD EXAMPLES

So are there any CV templates or examples that I would recommend? Well, **www.cvtemplate.co.uk**, despite the name, isn't really a template site but an online CV builder site, which is intuitive and easy to use, and the CV examples at **www.cvexamples.co.uk** are of better quality than the norm. If you really want to use CV examples then you are better off using something like these than poor quality examples.

At the same time, I should point out that another major flaw with using CV templates and examples is that they tend to lull the job seeker into a false impression. Even if you use the best quality examples, I should reiterate that this doesn't necessarily mean that you will get the best CV. If you want the best results then you need an original high-impact CV which is flexibly written based around you, your circumstances and the job in question.

Elsewhere in this book I elaborate on how this can be achieved.

PREFERRED FORMAT

If you want to have a look at my preferred format please feel free to check out this page: **http://www.cvsucceed.co.uk/our-cv-example/** Please note that the example on that page is exactly that: namely, an example. Pretty much by definition therefore it won't be specific enough to be appropriate for you personally without amendments pertaining to your own experience, circumstances and the target job.

That said, my preferred format is tried and tested, and gets great results. One of the reasons why it works is that it has an excellent vertical and horizontal words-to-space ratio which helps get your message across more effectively. Not only this, but among other things it was very well perceived by employers and professionals during my tests. Of course, any format is subjective to some degree, and beauty is in the eye of the beholder and all that. Nevertheless, if it came top in the tests, people like it, and it gets results, then surely there must be something in it.

HANG ON – WHAT ABOUT THE SHEEP?

If you are still reading then you almost certainly are not one of those sheep who just copy examples without much thought. So don't worry, an overzealous border collie won't come snapping at your heels. Besides he is already busy rounding up those bleaters who dashed out earlier at the prospect of flashy desks and big fat cigars.

3

Pre-write foresight

Foolish writers and readers are created for each other.

HORACE WALPOLE

... how to prepare before you even start writing your CV. And yes I did say *prepare* ...

Thinking about the above quotation, maybe Horace was referring to conventional CV books when he said that. I certainly don't see the wisdom in simply recycling flawed and outdated material from other books (as other CV authors seem to do) then cajoling the reader into making the same old mistakes.

I hope by now you are beginning to realise that I'm not a typical CV writer, this book isn't a standard book, and, since you have had the foresight to buy it, you are not your average reader either!

Unmasking the unasked

So while we are in the moment, let us get stuck straight in – or rather, the exact opposite. I did warn you that the CV was an enigmatic beast!

The first thing I want you to do with your CV (somewhat paradoxically), is simply to forget about it for the time being. Don't worry, we'll come back to the slippery so-and-so soon enough, but before we get ahead of ourselves, let us first of all get our heads around the real and significant question: what do you want your CV to do?

It's a simple enough question, but one which goes unasked, let alone unanswered by millions of people all over the world. Too many people jump the gun and hurriedly start scribbling their life story before they have even considered the whys and wherefores.

You may have possibly even done this yourself in the past? Well perhaps previously, but not any more ...

Pre-write foresight action

Hands-on session

So, reborn CV aficionado, let's get cracking. While your CV is safely tucked out of sight in your sock drawer, I would like you to take a blank piece of paper (hopefully from a different drawer) and just write down the answers to a few simple questions:

- What job are you targeting?
- Is it one job (or job type) in particular? Or are you open-minded?
- Is it something you have experience in?
- Or is it more of a career change?
- What kind of skills, qualifications and experience do employers for that job look for?
- What kind of people do employers in that sector look for?
- Is there anything you can bring to the table over and above your competitors?

There we go, that was quite painless wasn't it? And a lot easier than writing a personal profile, or refining cluttered paragraphs down to neat single line high-impact bulleted achievements (patience, my friend).

Even so, as easy as it was, you have just taken a significant and important step in creating a better CV.

While I wouldn't start popping champagne corks just yet, congratulations are still in order because you have just achieved something more than hundreds, thousands, if not millions of job seekers don't: namely, started distancing yourself, your ego and your preconceptions from your CV and instead started thinking in terms of what is actually required for a successful application.

You may not have realised it as you were doing it, but the list you have just made is important. While it is not, and never will be, a CV, it is a very good point of reference nevertheless, and you can certainly use it to help create a more effective CV. At many points in this book I will mention the term *'relevant'*. It is a very important term in CV language, and if you are ever unsure about whether or not something is relevant, I want you to refer back to your newly drafted list – it is there for good reason.

Regardless of what you do with your old CV – scribble over it, scrunch it up, or sizzle the brute in a frustrated blowtorch tussle – I would like you to keep hold of your lovely new list, and treat it with care and reverence. It's your friend. A good little elf, to prod your side, tug your sleeve and keep you plodding along in the right direction.

Your new CV canvas

If you succeed in considering the employer while selling *yourself* then you have half a chance. But if you ignore the employer and write standardised general rhetoric then you may as well just scrunch up your CV and save yourself a stamp.

As with all aspects of CV writing, 'considering the employer' is easier said than done, and the vast majority of people underestimate just how hard it is to get right. I hope the lessons I have learnt over many years of experience will help you.

The following chapters will enable you to write a CV better than any other advice book, and they do so not by giving you useless generic examples and inviting you to copy them parrot-fashion. On the contrary, if you truly want the best CV for *you*, then *you* will need to be able to think for yourself, and consider a Pandora's box full of posers, factors and issues. Not only this, but you will need to be able to resolve these issues if you want the best results.

I will be totally upfront with you at this point, and candidly state that this is far from easy and, regardless of what anyone says, you aren't going to write a top quality CV in the blink of an eyelid or at the touch of a button. You need to crawl before you can walk, and walk before you can run. Yes, this book can help you hop, skip and jump right up the career ladder if it is where you want to go, but it's a bit of a two-way thing, and here's the deal: I do my bit and explain how to improve your CV beyond recognition, and you do your bit and put down that glass, turn off the TV ('*but it's Emmerdale*' – I know), and go and grab yourself a pencil. To paraphrase a famous TV character, '*We are going to do the best day's (or several evenings, if need be) work you've ever done, Mr O'Reilly of Wobble Wall Terrace, Torquay!*'

Besides, you can always catch the *Emmerdale* omnibus on Sunday.

So, if you are happy to accept all that, and are ready to proceed, let's go about whipping your CV into the best shape of its life.

The first thing I want you to do is empty your mind of your previous preconceptions about what a CV should include, exclude, look like, mention and do. Most people's preconceptions are built on the shaky foundations of CV-writing myth rather than anything solid or useful. And if you really want to achieve your goal you need to be flexible, open-minded and creative.

Were you thinking about getting out your current CV? Forget it. We need to think big, think fresh, think better. And to do that we need a brand new canvas.

So before we do anything else, let's just take a moment to sit back and picture your CV. Now imagine a big eraser rubbing it out until nothing is left but a blank white page.

Talking of goals – take a while to consider just what the goals of writing a CV are anyway:

- Telling the employer about your work history?
- Making sure you target the job?
- Keeping everything neat, tidy and presentable?
- Selling your skills?

Actually it is all of these things, but at the same time none of them. Pandora's box is indeed an enigma.

Who are you aiming at?

If I had an argument with a player we would sit down for twenty minutes, talk about it and then decide I was right! BRIAN CLOUGH

... focusing your CV is a key element if you want to target your applications properly for jobs. This section should give you an important grounding in the subject – with more to follow later...

TAKE AIM AND FIRE

In fact, the ultimate purpose of any CV is to get you an interview (which, as long as you perform well at interview, should hopefully turn into a job).

Amazingly, an incredible number of people seem to forget this, and instead concentrate their efforts on simply trying to get their CV to conform to sets of artificial myths, rather than concentrating on turning it into something which is going to grab the employer's attention, and make him or her sit up and take notice.

Sometimes the best way forward is indeed a conventional way, but you also need to be intelligent, lucid and flexible enough to realise that sometimes you may also need to come from a different angle, and take a different approach if you want to have the best chance of landing a particular job.

This reminds me of something Brian Clough said in his autobiography. The story relates to when Brian was taking his football coaching badge and the person in charge was trying to teach Brian (one of the most prolific goal-scorers this country has ever seen) how to score from crosses. In his own inimitable way Brian went on to recount how he was told that the way to score from crosses was with his forehead, whereas Brian's argument was that it didn't really matter how he did it as long as he achieved his ultimate target: namely, scoring a goal. So instead of scoring with his forehead Brian went on to score with pretty much every other part of his body, proving in the process that if you are open-minded and flexible you can achieve your target – probably far more effectively in his case than if he had restricted himself to just one conventional method of trying to reach his goal.

If you want to achieve your career ambitions then the book you are reading can help you like no other – just don't expect the same old *'forehead'* rhetoric as advocated in other books. If you really want to achieve your job goals as successfully as Brian scored his, then you may well need to follow his example and use your initiative, creativity, and other methods or means at your disposal.

This may sound daunting, but don't worry, I'll be helping you on your way. Keep listening ...

4

Unlocking the secrets

By three methods may we learn wisdom: first, by reflection, which is noblest; second, by imitation, which is easiest; and third, by experience, which is the bitterest. CONFUCIUS

... there is a lot of advice out there – much of it contradictory and not thought out. This chapter will help you better identify the good, the bad, and if not the ugly, then at least the unhelpful and unfathomable.

This chapter should not only help you understand the art of CV writing all the more, but the hands-on sessions should also help you put things into practice too. To help you identify CV rights and wrongs I've also included ticks (right), crosses (wrong) and question marks (possibles/grey areas).

Rules v guidelines

The golden rule is that there are no golden rules.
MAN AND SUPERMAN (GEORGE BERNARD SHAW)

Elsewhere in this book I highlight examples of CV-writing myths. There are other fallacies too, masquerading as rules. The main thing to remember is to use your common sense. If you are having trouble writing a particular part of your CV because a so-called rule doesn't make sense, then sometimes it makes sense to question the rule rather than your sanity.

A lot of CV *rules* should not really be rules at all because if you follow a rule it may do you more harm than good. There are however, some simple *guidelines* that are worth following. But even some of these are not rigid and can be bent slightly should the need arise.

CVS SHOULD HAVE A PROFESSIONAL NOT HUMOROUS TONE

This is actually one CV rule which on the whole I agree with. Try to be too clever and you will usually become unstuck. For example:

- *'I bring ignorance to the table'*
- *'I can taste success on my spit when I get up in the morning'*

These are just two of several comments James McQuillan, a candidate on BBC's *The Apprentice,* made on his application. Not surprisingly James was subsequently derided for these comments. There is a time and a place for everything and, while I wouldn't rule out humour for certain applications, when you apply for a job with a hard-nosed businessman such as Lord Sugar it probably isn't the best time to joke around.

 ## KEEPING YOUR CV JARGON FREE

Again this is something which I largely agree with, and I'd have given the section a nice big tick if it were not for the fact that a small amount of commonly recognised jargon probably won't do much harm – as long as it really is just a small amount and the reader should understand what you mean.

Having worked on a great many CVs over the years, I actually have a pretty good feel for some of the jargon and technical terminology used in different professions. However, even I have to look things up sometimes and it is not only pretty frustrating, but also nonsensical. People who saturate their CVs with jargon usually think they are being clever, whereas in reality they are only being too clever for their own good. Most HR executives are not technical people, and they are really more concerned about you and what you can do for them, not what acronyms you know, and all the ins and outs of 2GL programming.

 ## BEING HONEST ON YOUR CV

This is something I certainly agree with. And if you watch pro-grammes like *The Apprentice* you will know that many candidates come unstuck and lose out on good jobs because they have been less than candid on their CV. If you are good enough for the job then you shouldn't have to lie to get it. Fair enough, you're not going to be shoved on the stand and have a Bible plonked in your hands *'straight up Your Honour ...'* and nor will your average employer strap you to a chair, attach electrodes, and tut in disgust each time the little needle thing causes more than the slightest blimp on the printout graph. Even so, it's better to be honest and upfront – if not to avoid the trouble and the embarrassment of getting found out then for your own peace of mind.

That said, while honesty is the best policy, sometimes it does pay to be a bit creative (see below).

？ THE TRUTH THE WHOLE TRUTH AND NOTHING BUT THE TRUTH

While I agree that you should tell the truth in your CV, you are not obliged to say *everything*. I would like to be clear about this: I do not mean that you should lie, but when you write your CV you do not necessarily have to say every part of the truth.

Many CVs are far too long and say far too much just because the writer has chosen to include every last bit of information, including all school grades, every job and every single interest from stamp collecting to Kung Fu. In such cases the employer may appreciate your honesty, but it is more likely that they would be rather nonplussed at the excessive and irrelevant content. Some people make the mistake of thinking that the more they write the more impressed an employer will be. This could not be further from the truth. Top CV writers know what to leave out as well as what to include, and if you want to impress then you too need to be very selective and strike the right balance.

Bending and bending

I think I should be clear about the terminology here. By *'bending'* I do not mean deliberately adding false entries or fictitious claims. That would be wrong. What is sometimes helpful, however, is to change or omit something which detracts from your cause. Sometimes it pays to be a little bit creative.

For example, if you have had many jobs in the past and do not want to appear as a job hopper then there are techniques you can use to portray your situation more favourably without being dishonest. As mentioned elsewhere, you can change or exclude obvious irrelevant entries, you can combine jobs, and you can tweak the dates where there are overlaps.

Top ten CV tips

All of us, at certain moments of our lives, need to take advice and to receive help from other people.
ALEXIS CARREL

I am regularly asked to give tips on CV writing. I've already given some in this book, and there are lots more to follow. However, to help you on your way, I've listed ten very useful tips below.

X 1 DO NOT UNDERESTIMATE THE VALUE OF YOUR CV

On the contrary, you should be very aware that your CV is one of the most important documents in your possession. How good (or bad) it is could dictate just how far you go (or stagnate) in your career.

2 BE METICULOUS

Employers have been known to discount CVs on the basis of small spelling or grammatical errors, but really any minor slip-ups can count against you so it is best to go through your CV with a fine-tooth comb, and check everything. For example, even formatting and alignment are significant. If something isn't aligned properly the presentation will be affected adversely, which in turn weakens first impressions.

3 DON'T UNDERESTIMATE THE IMPORTANCE OF GOOD CONTENT

Don't think that just because your CV includes all your work experience and appears presentable that is enough to get employers to take notice. Many of your competitors will also have presentable CVs. You need to go way beyond this if you are to stand out.

 ## 4 SELL YOURSELF

Remember that your CV is a sales document; you are selling yourself to the employer. Any Tom, Dick or Harry can list their work experience and most employers will have piles of CVs on their desk from people listing just that. You need to go beyond the average and sell yourself not only effectively, but also powerfully if you really want to grab the employer's attention.

 ## 5 DON'T SELL YOURSELF SHORT

Some people know they need to sell themselves, but are nevertheless overly modest on their CV. Some of my clients are at the top of their profession, but are still reluctant to extol their own virtues; partly because they think they may come across as 'big-headed'. If this applies to you, then you should not be afraid to sell yourself, and especially if you have genuine skills and traits to tout.

 ## 6 PORTRAY YOURSELF AS AN ACHIEVER

Employers look for achievers; your CV needs to stand out over and above the competition. That said, if you do show off your skills, you need to do so realistically, and back up your claims with examples where possible.

? 7 THINK OUTSIDE THE BOX IF NEED BE

Sometimes your application can be enhanced with a bit of creativity and original thinking. I'm not talking about folding your CV into a giant love heart shape before sending it to Mr Sourpus, Manager at

Grumpy & Grumpier Recruitment Co.; it is usually best to remain professional about such things. But even so, there are still times when it pays to approach your application from a different angle.

X 8 DON'T UNDERESTIMATE THE VALUE OF YOUR COVER LETTER

The cover letter is an integral part of the job application process. The best cover letters are relevant and concise, and complement the CV rather than simply repeat it (as many people's do).

X 9 DON'T UNDO YOUR GOOD WORK WITH A POOR QUALITY PRINTOUT

If you have a good CV and cover letter don't spoil things by not printing them out properly. If you don't have a decent printer then it is worthwhile paying to have your documents printed properly on good quality paper.

? 10 BE WARY OF FRIENDLY *'ADVICE'*

Don't believe every bit of advice you are given. Now and again I hear that an adviser has advised someone to, for instance, over-elaborate each job, include irrelevant jobs and qualifications, write in cluttered paragraphs rather than neat bullet points, and add extra sections. One recruiter even told someone to add a section detailing *'non-relevant experience'*! While much of this advice is well-meaning, it is frequently misplaced.

You need to bear in mind, when asking an adviser for his or her opinion (especially the likes of some lesser recruiters), enquiring *'What do you think of my CV?'*, that that is a totally different approach to putting your CV among a pile of thirty or so others in front of an employer or HR executive and asking them *the* real *question they will be asking themselves* – which is not *'What do you think of this CV?'* but *'Is this the type of person we want working for us?'*

It is a very important and highly significant distinction.

The former is not exactly a loaded question. However, it not only invites but also actively encourages the reader to nitpick deliberately, and frequently to revert to their preconceptions on CV format. In practice, what usually happens is rather than give a valid and unbiased appraisal of how effective the CV reads for the job, the reader instead tends to personalise their response. Rather than putting themselves in the shoes of the employer, they instead point out what they see as discrepancies as compared with their own CV. Their starting point is frequently based on the premise that their own CV format is the standard-bearer for all formats, and anything different is bound to be inferior. Moreover, the very fact that someone has approached them for CV advice has the inevitable consequence of reinforcing the *adviser's* conviction that their format must be right, otherwise no one would come to them for an opinion. This leaves the door conveniently open for them to proclaim the wonders of their own format, safe in the knowledge that they are seen as an authority, and are therefore unlikely to be questioned.

It's all a bit of a circular process, and to my mind flawed.

When you go to someone for an opinion about your CV, rather than just accept the advice in its entirety you should really ask yourself questions along the lines of:

- Does the advice all make sense?
- Is that how the employer would really think?
- Is the advice based on facts or myths?
- Is the adviser a professional writer?
- How good is the adviser's own CV?
- If you put into practice all the advice what would be the result?

 ## 11 (ONE MORE FOR LUCK!) IF YOU NEED ASSISTANCE THEN SEEK HELP

If you are in doubt, get *good* professional advice. Your career is far too important to leave to chance. The job market is not a level playing field: some job seekers are far more proactive than others; some are naturally better at writing CVs; many use professional CV writers to gain a significant advantage. There are ways to gain an advantage yourself. Start by seeking free expert advice. Indeed, you can get a free appraisal at **www.cvsucceed.co.uk**

A surprising amount of so-called advice is actually contradictory if you try to implement it. Little wonder then that a significant number of people in the advisory business (such as recruiters and HR executives) use professional writers to write their CVs for them.

Sit (down and think) rep

Before we continue, I think it would be a useful exercise to take your nice fresh blank sheet of paper and start the task of creating your new CV. It is not going to be the finished article at this stage, so don't feel pressurised into dotting every 'i' and crossing every 't' just yet. Moreover, to get you started you can copy and paste some parts (hopefully the better bits) from your old CV onto this new virgin

page. At the same time (and bearing in mind what you have already just learned), what I would like you to do now is to start thinking about what you should be including, and what you should be leaving out. If you can also remember to keep the employer in mind, as well as keeping half an eye on things such as length and presentation, then that would be great, and fine for now.

We will go into these and other factors and issues in more detail later, but at this early stage it's all about focusing on creating something more relevant and more fit for purpose. You can amend/shape/mould it at your leisure as we move through the chapters of this book – and if you follow all the lessons, you should see a dramatic and much improved transformation at the end.

With that I'll give you an hour or so to let you get on with things. Have fun!

Dissecting the art of CV writing

The harder you work, the luckier you get. GARY PLAYER, GOLFER

... among other things that there is more to CV writing than most people (including other CV book authors/CV writers) realise ...

Welcome back – and I hope that you did indeed enjoy the experience, and I hope that your new CV is starting to look better, even at this early stage.

So, back to grabbing the employer's attention. The first thing you really need to know about this is that it doesn't happen by chance. Personally I take an almost scientific approach to CV writing. You can't just invent or pluck top-quality CVs out of thin air. You need structure, method and, yes, I really do believe you also need science to some degree.

In addition to that you also need a rounded understanding of some CV-writing basics. We'll tunnel deeper into the nitty-gritty later in the book, but first of all, let's do some more general groundwork.

Different CV types

It's not what you've got, it's what you use that makes a difference. ZIG ZIGLAR

I previously mentioned CV examples and, while these can be good or bad, even the better ones remain *examples* – no more than that – and if you choose to use a CV example then just remember that it will need changing. Bear in mind that just because it says 'Fork Lift Truck Driver' on the tin, it doesn't mean to say that all fork lift truck driver CVs need to be exactly like that – they don't.

In fact, contrary to what some people believe, there isn't a standard retail CV, a specific IT CV or a special accountant CV. In reality just as CVs come in all shapes, sizes, colours and formats, the same applies to CVs for particular sectors.

I mention this because now and again I receive enquiries from people with set ideas on what a CV in their particular sector should include and look like. This would be all well and good if everyone in that sector agreed, sharing exactly the same views. However, in reality this is never the case, and the CV format to which they are referring, although basically just one of many, happens to be the only one they are familiar with. This isn't too surprising as most people don't spend their time looking at lots and lots of different CVs. However, if they did they would realise that like mushrooms, flowers and insects there are a great many different varieties, even within the same genre.

For example, taking the IT sector: I have received IT CVs ranging from one to thirty pages, in a variety of colours, fonts, styles and formats. Some include photographs and logos, while most do not. Some include an objectives section, others a profile, and some have neither of these. Some are very basic, highlighting little more than a list of programs. On the other hand, some are extremely comprehensive, going into minute detail about familiarity with every single piece of hardware or software encountered throughout an entire career. Some include full and balanced skills and key competencies sections while others either have nothing at all or just have a more one-dimensional, brief technical list. Talking of technical, some IT CVs are extremely technical and full of acronyms and jargon, whereas others are nothing of the sort.

I could go on, but you get the gist; essentially it is something of a myth that there is a yardstick IT CV (or any CV type for that matter). And if someone told you there is, they really need to look at more CVs, because if they do that they would realise that this is nonsense.

The main reason I mention this is because now and again someone will change a perfectly good CV to incorporate something they mistakenly believe should be included on a so-called *representative* CV for their sector. Usually, this is pure nonsense, but for one reason or another they get it into their head that something is essential, so they add it, not with any logic in mind but simply to comply with a mistaken perception.

Career-change CVs

Don't let your luggage define your travels; each life unravels differently. SHANE KOYCZAN

Career-change CVs (i.e. changing jobs from one distinct career to another – say from a teacher to a salesperson), are arguably the most difficult to write. They are hard enough for professional writers to produce, and especially difficult for someone to write themselves.

Often when people contemplate writing a career-change CV they have limited (or sometimes no) experience in the new sector. Immediately therefore they are at a disadvantage compared with many of their competitors. After all, experience is a valuable commodity, and employers recognise this.

Nevertheless, it's not impossible to change direction or to break into a new career, it's just that bit harder (sometimes much harder depending

upon the sector). Regardless of the new job you intend targeting, one main prerequisite is that at the very least you can demonstrate some sort of aptitude for it. As mentioned, most people targeting a career change have limited or no experience in the new career sector, and this is problematic, unhelpful and frequently a bit of a conundrum. After all, if you are to compete effectively against people with more specialist experience then you need to do something not only to redress the balance, but also to tip it in your favour. This is no easy task, and is never a foregone conclusion. Indeed, sometimes you need to be honest enough to realise that breaking into particular careers without the prerequisite qualifications and experience just isn't going to happen. For example, there is no point applying for a job as a GP if you don't have any medical qualifications and are unwilling to study for them.

However, if you have experience working in a bank but would like to try your hand working in retail then the transition is more realistic and achievable. In such cases, one of the main things you need to do is highlight relevant transferable skills. For example, you could reinforce your numeric skills including your experience working with accounts and money. In addition to this you could also illustrate your office, administration and people skills, to name but three.

Essentially, what you need to do is understand what the new employer is looking for, and bring those skills to the table. If you can't do this via transferable skills from previous jobs, then sometimes you can call upon your academic achievements or voluntary experience to help demonstrate the skills, traits and experience the new employer is looking for.

This sounds very easy in theory, but it is always much harder in practice.

The reasons why it is harder revolve around natural tendencies. Over the years I have seen a great many attempts at DIY career-change CVs. Almost without exception these are not really fit for purpose, and wouldn't do the trick when put in front of a prospective employer. Indeed, one of the main reasons why we get so many career-change orders from clients is that their own attempts fail, and fail again. And one of the main reasons why these DIY CVs fail is because it's extremely difficult for someone to write their own career-change CV.

The vast majority of DIY career-change CVs I have seen aren't really that at all; they are general CVs with a few changes and some extra transferable skills. On the whole they do not address the new career properly, they do not highlight relevant skills as well as they need to, and ultimately they do not make any impact when it comes to competing against the CV of a more experienced specialist.

The most effective career-change CVs are actually radically different from the original ones. If you think about it logically, this has to be the case. I have lost count of the times when someone from a particular profession (e.g. marketing) sends me their CV and asks me why it never works when they apply for jobs in their new target sector (e.g. accounting). My response in such cases is almost always the same, for instance, *'Because it's aimed at marketing jobs and not at accounting jobs'*. And people do realise that they are doing this. Indeed their response is almost always along the lines of *'Yes, I know but I don't know how to change it'*.

This is exactly what I mean when I say that it is far harder for someone to write their own career-change CV. And one of the main reasons for this is because you need to come at it more objectively, from a different angle, and with a wider perspective. This is neither natural nor straightforward. If you are from a marketing background but want to change to accounting, then really you need a CV which is more in tune with the new sector. Not only this, but you also need to stress the right positives more effectively while addressing and successfully managing any negatives.

To exacerbate matters further, if you really want the best career-change CV then you also need to give it a lot more thought, care and attention. You also need to be prepared to spend far longer on it, writing more drafts, and meticulously refining it. When I write CVs I often write a draft then come back to it later with fresh eyes. When I write career-change CVs, I tend to do this far more often, as they often require many more drafts. You also need to be more open-minded and creative with career-change CVs.

Of course, it is entirely your prerogative how you go about things. But for what it's worth, if you are thinking of changing career and have written your own career-change CV then I would recommend getting a second opinion before sending it to employers. There are just some occasions when it is better to have someone else (for example a friend, colleague or, ideally, a professional) looking in from the outside more objectively. And career-change CVs fit into that bracket.

Standard-ish CVs

If there is anything the nonconformist hates worse than a conformist, it's another nonconformist who doesn't conform to the prevailing standard of nonconformity. BILL VAUGHAN

OH SO (UN)TYPICAL

While I am loath to describe anything CV as a *typical* CV (because frequently they are nothing of the sort), I think at the very least we can say that most people apply for jobs with a CV whose target at least partly matches up with the applicant's previous work experience. So for example, most people who are applying for accountancy jobs, tend to have financial experience (and in particular accountancy) among previous jobs listed on their CV.

The good news for all those job seekers who do have at least some previous relevant experience to draw from is that this not only adds weight to your applications, but also gives you something to focus on when you start improving your CV. The *'less good'* news is that (as you are perhaps coming to realise) there is more to making CV improvements than meets the eye. However, please have faith and keep reading – we'll get there slowly but surely.

In fact, we'll discover and examine CV nooks and crannies that you didn't even know existed – all in due course – but for now let's just examine some more familiar friends (or foes).

Personal profiles

Personality can open doors, but only character can keep them open. ELMER G. LETTERMAN

Contrary to what many people think, a CV personal profile is never going to be a deal-breaker, and it's never going to add as much weight to your applications as powerful, relevant, high-impact achievements. What a good profile can do, on the other hand, is give a striking initial impression, whet the employer's appetite, and entice him or her to sit up, take notice and read on.

That's what should happen. Unfortunately, many people put their foot in it when it comes to profile writing and, instead of socking it to the employer, find their applications are instead prematurely given the boot.

This is hardly surprising, because the profile is one of the hardest parts of your CV to write, and most people (including many professional writers) struggle with it.

Probably the biggest mistake people make is overcomplicating their profile; so instead of introducing themselves and laying the foundations for stating their case, they instead treat the profile like a mini CV, and try to cram as much into it as possible. Yes, I do realise that there are many advisers out there who will stick their beak in and try to henpeck you into doing just that. However, it doesn't make any sense, and it won't do you any favours. A profile is a profile; it isn't a canvas for your life history; it isn't a skills forum; it isn't a technical platform, and I repeat and reiterate it isn't a place where you just squash and summarise your CV either.

What a good profile should do is let the employer know, in clear and precise terms, that you are a specialist in the job that they are advertising, and that you look like you meet or surpass the criteria. If you can do that then you are preparing the groundwork to reel in the employer and give him or her a knockout punch in the achievements section. Try to be too clever for your own good, however, and it will be you, not anyone else, who comes crashing down all puffy-eyed and out for the count.

PERSONAL IMPROVEMENTS

So how can you go about improving your profile?

The first thing to do is make sure it is a good length. Personally (although I do have an open mind on this) I tend not to write profiles in excess of three lines. And if I have a preference then it is for two lines. Of course, I have years of experience writing concisely, so it is easier for me. You are new to this, so I can give you a bit of leeway (generous or what?). So if your profile is in excess of ... not two, not three but *four* lines, then the first thing I would like you to do is to refine it down to just four lines maximum. If you have trouble doing this then strike out anything that you think shouldn't really belong there.

Is it looking any better yet? I hope so.

X Another common mistake people make is that they write profiles which either don't flow, don't read well, or which just aren't logical in their progression. So the next thing I want you to do is read your profile out loud – if you stumble over the words, if it doesn't sound right then it probably isn't. If this is the case you will need to get tapping on that new laptop of yours and do a bit of resourceful touch-type tweaking.

✓ As a tip, one thing I've noticed is that a lot of people write start/stop profiles with very little flow. If you have a lot of full stops in your profile this may be hindering the flow, so consider that while you have your inventive hat on and are in Shakespeare mode.

Once you have refined your profile down so that it not only reads well but is four lines maximum, the next thing to do is to make sure that it is addressing the employer and his or her needs.

? Is it depicting you as a specialist? If not then one immediate thing you can do is put your job title in capital letters in the profile. For example: *HGV DRIVER*.

I know it's obvious, but if it is a direct match with the job specification then it's a good immediate indicator to the employer that the CV could be of potential interest, so it is worth doing.

What other kinds of things do employers look for?

Well, *experience* for starters, so you can include a reference to that. While you are at it you can also include several (but not all) relevant traits that the employer may want for the job in question. So, for an HGV driver it could be along the lines of the following:

> *A reliable class 1 C + E qualified HGV DRIVER with a clean driving licence and 20 years' accident-free experience driving lorries across Europe for major companies including FedEx.*

Previously, I mentioned the fact that formats vary a great deal in size, shape and quality. One important point of note here is that the above example is spread over three lines. So you have nearly used up the quota I gave you already. However, if you want to say quite a bit more while not eating too much into your vertical space, then this is possible if you use a different format. If you do that just be sure to use a format that is still neat and legible, rather than too cluttered. My preferred format for example, gives you more vertical space for your money. This can be put to good use by the inclusion of additional pertinent content. Assuming space allows, you could possibly add something along these lines:

A versatile and physically fit worker with yard shunting, strapping and trunking experience as well as the ability to work flexibly across multiple locations.

Some formats will allow you to combine both of the above examples into a presentable four- (or five-) line profile, which is still a decent length, even if it is slightly longer than I personally would normally use.

As you will note, the above example doesn't drag out the candidate's life history in 3D, DVD or flashing CV format, nor does it try to confuse the reader with PDP quotations or bits and bobs from their DPP record. All it really does is tell the HGV employer the kind of things that he or she want to know: *HGV licence, lots of experience* (including specialist areas such as *shunting/trunking/strapping*), *physically fit, flexible, accident free history,* etc.

I say '*all* it really does', but that is one very significant mama, and clearly highlighting a handful of relevant facts of undoubted interest to the employer is infinitely more effective than spouting one hundred thousand snippets of extraneous padding.

Informative as it is, the above profile alone probably won't get the candidate the job off its own steam, but it's certainly enough to whet the employer's appetite and entice him or her to read on, rather than sigh, make a paper aeroplane and trudge over to the next potential origami jet in the unread CVs pile.

I'm no expert on statistics, but somehow I suspect that the chances of you being a HGV driver are as slim – far slimmer than er ... well, most

HGV drivers as it happens. But this is neither here nor there, because regardless of your profession you can still learn from the above example, and you can still apply these lessons when it comes to writing your own personal profile.

POWER OF THE MIND

No prizes then for guessing what your next bit of homework is … Enjoy finishing your new profile!

Career history – an experience

We will be digging out our magnifying glasses and delving deeper into this section in due course, so I won't over-elaborate here. But for the time being, I just want to talk about the section in more global terms.

Essentially the work experience section is the most important part of your CV – or at least it should be if you have written it properly! A good, effective work experience section separates out the men from the boys, and the ladies from the lady-boys.

Ultimately, the employer is trying to assess several things on your CV, and top of the list are the questions *'Can you do the job?'* and *'Can you do the job better than anyone else?'*.

Most sections of the CV don't really give you the opportunity to answer these questions properly (and if you try to force the issue by attempting to answer them elsewhere then you are probably over-complicating matters). The work experience section, on the other hand, is the perfect medium for you to flex your achievements muscle – and really sock it to the employer that you are not only an achiever, but just the right achiever, and better than all the other candidates to boot.

There you go – told you it would be short and sweet – but don't think you're getting off that easily … magnifying glasses, more digging and hands-on sessions to follow – so enjoy the moment while it lasts!

Short course qualifications

Similarly, I discuss qualifications in more detail elsewhere, but taking a more global view for the time being here let's just say that the qualifications section is arguably the least thought about on most job seekers' CVs. Indeed, many people inadvertently turn their courses to a disadvantage rather than a plus point on their CV. Hopefully this won't apply to you, but even if it does we will help you identify potential problems and explain what you can do to fix and improve things later in this book.

Competencies section – a skill in itself

Your skills and competencies section should demonstrate just that: namely, skills and competencies. However, somewhat paradoxically, many people (including numerous advisers) somehow manage to do the exact opposite, and effectively just draw unwelcome attention to the fact that the one key skill in which they are seriously lacking is *written communications*. If you are applying for a job as a packer in a factory then this isn't the be all and end all. But just be aware that written (and oral) communication skills are highly valued by most employers in pretty much all job sectors, so if you don't state your case clearly and effectively then it hardly bodes well.

The irony is that the skills section should be one of the easiest sections to write on your whole CV, and the trick is to not overcomplicate matters. Simple enough you may think, but you would be surprised just how many people try to multiply administration skills by Σ^2 then divide by the capital of Venezuela.

Totally Caracas I know!

Hands-on session

Anyway, let's get back to the task of helping you improve your own skills section.

The first thing to do is get rid of any dead wood if need be. So, if someone (I don't know, perhaps a lesser recruiter?) had previously told you to include a core skills section, a technical skills section and a personal skills section, then I would like you simply to strike out anything which doesn't seem particularly appropriate to the job you are targeting, then condense what is left into just one section. You can give it the header *'skills and key competencies'*. (Please note that *competencies* are more natural/personal traits whereas *skills* relate more to specialities that you learn over time with experience. It is good to include both because employers actually consider both when they are weighing up whether or not you are up to the job and are the right fit for their organisation.)

Hopefully, most of you won't have had to delete too much, but some people reading this right now will be left with just their name, contact details and a conspicuously big gaping hole on a predominantly blank page. But that's okay, pretty much everyone reading this book will need to rewrite their CV from scratch (rather than just tweak things) if they want the best results anyway.

Assuming that you personally do have some skills left on your CV, how many are there? And perhaps more appropriately, how much space do they take up? If your skills are still hogging your CV then something is amiss. While skills are an integral part of your CV, they are still a relative bit player in the whole scheme of things. So refine them down yet further if need be.

Once you have a list of relevant skills, the next thing to do is to make them more proactive. For example, an HGV driver might have a skills list which includes the following:

- driving lorries
- loading
- yard strapping
- European routes

These are all well and good, and HGV employers should appreciate such entries. Even so, with a bit of tweaking they can be made even better. For example, 'driving lorries' can become '20 years' lorry driving experience', and 'European routes' can be improved to 'Considerable European route knowledge'. You get the gist.

If the skills on your current CV are on the basic side (as many are), then you could beef up your own CV along the same lines.

Why not have a go at this right now? If so, you could add 'keen and enthusiastic' to your list of competencies!

As mentioned, you should be careful not to overdo things, or make your skills section complicated. It should be neat, straightforward, and easy for any employer to just quickly skim through and get a good feel of the kind of skills and personal characteristics you bring to the table.

If yours doesn't do that yet then you should head back to the drawing board before thinking about bounding over to the table with a clumsily cobbled together box of tricks.

I know what some of you are thinking;

- 'Where should I put the skills section?'
- 'What do you mean by *relevant* skills?'
- 'What if I am a technical person?'
- 'How do I refine things down?'

These questions are all answered elsewhere in this book.

Reviving your CV

I have left orders to be awakened at any time in case of national emergency, even if I'm in a cabinet meeting. RONALD REAGAN

WAKEY-WAKEY

So how do you grab the employer's attention and stir him or her into action? Well, first and foremost you need to be better than your competitors on several fronts, and stress your relevant positives more comprehensively, more eloquently and ultimately more effectively than they do.

This may sound quite daunting given the number of applicants per job, but the vast majority of people don't sell themselves properly,

and most don't think about targeting their CV anywhere near as much as they need to. So, on the positive side, the vast majority of the competition isn't up to much.

Unfortunately, however, this still leaves a significant minority whose CVs certainly are up to the job, and it is these people you need to beat rather than the masses. It is impossible to quantify such things with any real precision, but I would say that around 30 per cent of the DIY CVs I get asked to rewrite are very poor to begin with, and around 65 per cent are reasonable or even quite good but still pretty much run-of-the-mill in the whole scheme of things. This leaves a small percentage of DIY CVs which are relatively good, and, in addition to the DIY CVs, there is a fair chance that you will be competing against good professional CVs too.

Think about how many CVs will be considered – will you make the cut? It would be all well and good if every employer took on 20 per cent of applicants. However, in the real world it is usually just one winner per job on offer. The odds therefore are not particularly good. Saying that, they are not insurmountable either, especially considering that a large proportion of your competition will underestimate the importance of their CV, and certainly won't give it anywhere near as much attention as necessary.

The very fact that you are reading this book is a clear indication that you are taking your CV seriously, and the sections below should serve to enlighten you further.

Spotting a good CV

We've established that you need to grab the employer's attention. With that in mind, take a look at the following two CVs and, before you read on, answer these questions. Which is the best CV? How good is it? Is it better/worse than yours? Why/why not?

CV1

JOE BLOGGS
94 Church Row, York • Email joe83@jb.com • Tel. (01632)960871

EXPERIENCE

2006–Present   ABC CORPORATION, YORK
Analyst
- Research & conduct investigations and analysis as part of a large business and development team
- Conduct extensive research and build up business case for investment
- Work closely alongside a wide range of clients on projects including a new corporate database
- Work on a range of functions from finance to research and development
- Meet with management teams and attend numerous meetings in the UK and abroad
- Develop business, growth and marketing strategies for a variety of companies across the country

2003–2006   DEFG CORPORATION, LONDON
Sales Executive
- Sold a variety of products and services from computers to training solutions
- Secured new clients both in London and around the home counties
- Awarded salesmen of the month three times in a 12 month period

2002–2003   HIJ COMPANY, YORK
TEFL Teacher
- Taught English as a foreign language to students
- Worked in several countries including France, Germany, Japan and Sweden
- Helped develop new training material to aid student progress

---

EDUCATION
2001   Bachelor of Arts Degree in Music, York University

PERSONAL
Interests include: Music • Tennis • Biking • Reading • Travel

---

CV2

JOE BLOGGS
1 Church Row, York y022 2hg ♦ Mob: 07700 900888 ♦ Email: joe83@jb.com

INTERNATIONAL SALES MANAGER

Exposure to Multiple Industries & Sales functions

———————————————— AREAS OF EXPERTISE ————————————————

Sales Development & Growth   Client Services   After sales
Advertising   Sales Proposals   Negotiation
Promotions   Consultative Selling Approach Multilingual

———————————————— PROFESSIONAL EXPERIENCE ————————————————

ABC Ltd, York   2000 to Present

SALES MANAGER

➤ Was recruit to find and sell IT products to clients across the UK, USA and
  EEMEA region.
➤ Worked effectively with sales and marketing teams at a number of locations
➤ Met sales targets
➤ Won salesman of the year award in 2004

———————————————— EDUCATION & CERTIFICATIONS ————————————————

➤ York high school – seven GCSEs

———————————————— INTERESTS ————————————————

➤ Sport, music, football, painting

What do you think? Which one is the best? And how good is it? Good? Average? Poor? Have a look at them again before answering.

My answer to the question would be: while the second CV is certainly flawed in as much as it has spelling and grammatical errors, formatting problems and is very bare/basic, it nevertheless has a far greater chance of making an impact on an employer than the first CV.

Yes, the first CV is more comprehensive, is grammatically superior and is arguably better formatted. Yet in spite of this, it is no use to anyone. Admittedly, it does some things reasonably well. For example, it makes good use of bullet points and the legibility factor is high. Additionally, at first glance it may seem more impressive because the achievements have more to them, and the candidate has better qualifications etc. However, in order to assess how effective the CV is, you need first of all to put yourself in the employer's shoes, and ask yourself the very same question the employer would ask himself or herself: namely, 'What can this person do for me?'

Significantly, as far as the first CV is concerned the answer to this question is that ... it is impossible to say!

How can a prospective employer possibly evaluate how good this candidate is for his or her organisation? The CV is so generic that you don't even know what job this person is targeting. Not only that but you don't even know where his real expertise truly lies.

Both CVs could be better, but at least the second CV has addressed some of the basic fundamentals and has some focus and direction, and at the very least a potential employer can see that the candidate is a specialist salesperson with experience. The first CV, on the other hand, is in No Man's Land and really poses more questions than it delivers answers. It is certainly not going to make an employer rush to the phone to arrange an interview.

What about your new, developing CV? Did you succumb to any of the potential pitfalls? Is it well formatted? How legible is it? Is it grammatically perfect? Could you express yourself more clearly? Is it specific and targeted? Is it too general/generic? Does it have the right direction?

Imagine for a minute that your CV will be landing on discerning employer, Lord Sugar's desk. Honestly, do you really think your CV is going to make him bounce his eyebrows, sport an interested grin, and lick his lips in eager anticipation of you turning up to his office to tell him more of the same?

If not you could be in trouble. Luckily I can help you.

Fitting the pieces together

… a riddle wrapped in a mystery inside an enigma.
WINSTON CHURCHILL, ON RUSSIA

So how do you add focus and direction to your CV? Well, one of the first things you can do is to realise the difference between versatility and specialisation.

A surprising number of people make the mistake of thinking that *'more is more'*. This may be well and good if we were talking about something quantifiable such as lollipops or ice creams. However, written documents are not the same, and sometimes *'less is more'*.

To illustrate this, just put yourself in the eyes of an employer for a moment and consider this: if you had two CVs on your desk in front of you, one of which was four pages long and included every last detail of the candidate's entire education and work history, and the other was half the size, but concisely summarised all the relevant information, which one would you choose to read first?

I am sure that most of you will say the latter, and significantly most employers would probably reach for the more concise CV first too.

Relevant and concise CVs don't just score brownie points on grabbing the employer's attention, they are usually more effective once the employer actually starts reading too.

You know yourself that if you pick up a book or magazine and the content is well written and of interest to you then you will continue reading. However, if it comes across as repetitive, irrelevant or padded out then you are far more likely just to give up the ghost, and put it down for a more interesting read. CVs which try to say too much tend to have this effect on employers. People forget that employers are busy people, too busy to be interested in the fact that you have done a lot of different courses which have nothing whatsoever to do with the job on offer, far too busy to be interested in the fact that you did a paper round when you were 15 years old, and certainly far too busy to be told for the umpteenth time in the same CV that you have basic MS Excel skills.

Okay, so I may be exaggerating a bit here: not everybody lists reams of irrelevant courses and most people have the sense to omit the inclusion of their paper round. That said, pretty much every single CV I have ever rewritten for a client has involved removing superfluous or irrelevant content from their original. So if you are sat here reading this thinking that these issues do not apply to you, then at the very least I would urge you to think again, because unless you are very much the exception to the rule, such issues could well apply to your CV to one degree or another.

Either way we will find out, as we will explore this later in one of the practical sessions.

Of course, you can always be an eager beaver and get your sharp gnashers into some CV pruning practice before you get that far.

A shiny gold star for my golden star pupil if you do!

Strengthening your message

Sometimes the questions are complicated and the answers are simple. DR SEUSS

… everyone knows they need a strong sales message on their CV (well, most people do anyway). This section should enlighten you and help you to dramatically bolster your own sales message …

 SIMPLY THE BEST

Have you ever wondered why most menus are uncluttered and relatively simple? Have you noticed that the best websites tend to have straightforward, easy-to-follow navigation?

These are not coincidences, but the results of deliberate commercial strategies based on the absolute fact that too much text is a turn-off, and that if you want to entice a prospective buyer to read something (remember an employer is prospectively buying your services) then it not only needs to be interesting, relevant and enticing, it also needs to be legible, presentable and sufficiently concise.

When marketing companies create expensive poster campaigns they tend to work on a maximum ten-words-per-poster rule. With all the costs involved in promotional campaigns, you can be sure that if global marketing companies have strict word-count policies when it comes to selling their products, then they do this for good reason.

If blue-chip marketing companies value the importance of concise focused messages when it comes to selling their products then at the very least they should serve as a good indication that there must be something in it. And of course there is; you only need to look at the packaging on the covers of the most popular products to see that the message is usually very straightforward, clear and attractive.

If you want to sell yourself to employers then you really need to work along the same lines and deliver an unambiguous focused message. You also need to remember that the more things you add over and above your initial message, and the more you complicate matters, then the more diluted and weak your main message ultimately becomes.

EASY AS 123 ...

The generation of random numbers is too important to be left to chance. ROBERT R. COVEYOU, OAK RIDGE NATIONAL LABORATORY

Now obviously your CV can't be restricted to ten words, but the rule of brevity still applies. If your CV looks cluttered and uneasy on the eye then this is a clear sign that there is something wrong. The same applies if it is too bare. Really you should be looking for a happy medium: namely, a CV which makes good use of space, and sells your skills in a presentable fashion without too much clutter. If you manage that then you are probably on the right track.

What you will need to keep in mind is that different CV formats, styles and fonts will also have a bearing on how many words you can fit on a page: while 400 words of one font could fill up one page in a particular format, the same 400 words could fill up two pages in a slightly different font and format.

With that in mind, let's have another look at your own CV. How does it measure up?

Don't think too hard about it – remember first impressions count. Just take it out of the drawer, have a quick glance, and decide in an instant whether or not it looks fine, is on the cramped side, or is need of a trip to the CV barbers.

If it is more of a perturbed psychic than the happy medium I mentioned above then don't worry too much – I'm used to all that and will introduce you to solutions that should put you in fine spirits later in this book.

Generic v speciality

Your problems and mine are nothing new, they are all just another small part of the generic nightmare. LEWIS WARD

... how to make your CV far more relevant – something which ultimately plays a big part when it comes to grabbing the employer's attention ...

JACK AND JILTED

Returning to my point about versatility and specialism: when most people go job-hunting they usually have a fairly open mind in as much as if their first choice job does not materialise then they would happily consider a reasonable alternative. In view of this, a great many people deliberately create CVs which are versatile.

Part of the reason behind this is the natural temptation for people to sound off about each and every string to their bow, thinking that this will impress the employer. And while employers do appreciate versatility, in reality they are usually looking for specialists, rather than jacks of all trades.

So while the natural impulse is to create an all-purpose, all-encompassing generic CV which shows off a broad range of skills, traits and experience, really this isn't the best way forward.

When you send off a job application you are not entering a *'Who's got the most skills?'* competition. Instead you should be concentrating on trying to convince the employer that you are a specialist in the job he or she has on offer, and can do everything he or she is looking for, better than all your competitors.

Put it another way: if the electrics go on your house, and you get offers to fix them from two people, (1) a fully qualified specialist electrician, and (2) a builder whose main experience is building extensions but who nevertheless has some experience across a range of skills including masonry, plumbing, electrics and tiling – who would you choose?

I think it is safe to say that most people would choose the specialist electrician. Yes, a versatile builder could prove useful, but if people want a particular job done well then most would prefer to engage a specialist.

This is significant because employers think on exactly the same lines when it comes to employing someone to fill a specific vacancy. Yes, you could try to cover all bases with a very generic CV, but if you do so you risk losing out to a specialist.

It is all common sense really, but you would be surprised to see just how many people are applying for administration jobs with CVs which portray them as a financial whiz kid salesperson with graphic design skills and experience across tourism, agriculture and chemical engineering.

You may think I am joking, and admittedly it is an exaggeration, but the exaggeration is built on a solid base of fact. While I'm not suggesting that your own CV portrays you as a *Financial Times* reading agricultural tour rep/salesperson/chemist, at the very least I think I can say in all confidence that if every single person reading this right now looked again at their CV (you too – hint, hint!), then a high proportion will have CVs which are not optimised or focused enough towards a specific specialism. If you don't fall into this category then I congratulate you, you are a happy exception to the rule.

Reverse generic engineering

Hands-on session

I think at this point it would be useful to revisit one of the two CV examples I listed previously. It would be a good exercise to examine it again and see if we could tweak it to make it more focused. I've shown the CV again opposite.

To give you a jump start for this exercise, I'll set the ball rolling by making the assumption that I've spoken to Mr Bloggs (thoroughly good bloke), and it transpires he has made a list of his own and he has decided that he is now looking to concentrate on sales.

Any ideas about what we can do to help Joe out?

There is no need to scrutinise the CV under the microscope or dissect it letter by letter, but if you can just jot down some ideas on a piece of paper that will do for this practical session, and longer term it could well help you when it comes to focusing your own CV – so please don't dismiss it. On the contrary, get stuck in and have a go.

Well, I hope that this poser in black and white got the old grey matter churning and you've had the odd brainwave or two sparking up potential illuminating improvements.

What did you do? Was it constructive? Inspired? Or did it just involve a cork or ring pull? The former two I hope.

Anyway, before you dash off for a refill, let's quickly move on and identify some of the main things you could have done to help.

For starters, you could have included a personal profile which concentrates on sales. We will learn more about personal profiles later.

JOE BLOGGS
94 Church Row, York • Email joe83@jb.com • Tel. (01632)960871

EXPERIENCE

2006–Present   ABC CORPORATION, YORK

Analyst
- Research & conduct investigations and analysis as part of a large business and development team
- Conduct extensive research and build up business case for investment
- Work closely alongside a wide range of clients on projects including a new corporate database
- Work on a range of functions from finance to research and development
- Meet with management teams and attend numerous meetings in the UK and abroad
- Develop business, growth and marketing strategies for a variety of companies across the country

2003–2006   DEFG CORPORATION, LONDON

Sales Executive
- Sold a variety of products and services from computers to training solutions
- Secured new clients both in London and around the home counties
- Awarded salesmen of the month three times in a 12 month period

2002–2003   HIJ COMPANY, YORK

TEFL Teacher
- Taught English as a foreign language to students
- Worked in several countries including France, Germany, Japan and Sweden
- Helped develop new training material to aid student progress

---

EDUCATION
2001   Bachelor of Arts Degree in Music, York University

PERSONAL
Interests include: Music • Tennis • Biking • Reading • Travel

---

Another option would be to have restructured the work experience section so that it plays up the sales experience, and plays down the other, less relevant experience.

You may have also thought about adding a skills section that included some attributes relevant to sales.

If you did some or all of these things you could have possibly ended up with amendments along the lines shown overleaf.

JOE BLOGGS
94 Church Row, York • Email joe83@jb.com • Tel. (01632)960871

PROFILE
A confident, friendly, award-winning SALESMAN with excellent interpersonal skills and a proven record achieving demanding sales targets for a leading IT company

---

EXPERIENCE
2006–Present   ABC CORPORATION, YORK
Analyst
- Developed successful sales & marketing strategy as analyst for a top UK firm
- Built excellent relations with clients and stakeholders at all levels

2003–2006   DEFG CORPORATION, LONDON
Sales Executive
- Won three salesmen of the month awards in just 12 months for a top IT company
- Commended for in-depth knowledge across a range of products and IT services
- Secured new clients both in London and the home counties, boosting profits
- Successfully negotiated a £200,000 software contract with *Stevenage FE College*
- Prepared bids & presented to NHS directors to secure a £400k training contract

2002–2003   HIJ COMPANY, YORK
TEFL Teacher
- Sold courses and taught students in France, Germany, Japan and Sweden

---

EDUCATION
2001   Bachelor of Arts Degree in Music, York University

SKILLS & KEY COMPETENCIES
- Extensive multichannel sales skills
- Proven closing ability at board level
- Excellent communication and presentation skills
- Confident and friendly communicator
- Ambitious, reliable and motivated

Of course you can't just make up new achievements off the top of your head, and you can't include them if they are not true, but I've had a friendly chinwag with Joe, and he filled me in on some things he left out. As it transpires, he is much better at sales than his initial CV intimated.

As you can see, the previous general CV is now a lot more focused towards the sales target. It still needs work, and there are still lots of things we can do to improve it yet further (and we will come to these in turn in due course).

✓ Adapting to adaptability – job specifications

Adapt or perish, now as ever, is nature's inexorable imperative. H.G. WELLS

One such thing you can do revolves around adapting your CV where appropriate.

I have talked about the need to be flexible, and on an individual, *horses-for-courses* basis. Among other things I have introduced ideas on how to consolidate and consequently improve your CV. However, first and foremost you need to get the fundamentals right: length, presentation, legibility. These are the building blocks around which you can construct the rest of your CV. And the only way to be able to fit all the pieces together properly is if you adopt an adaptable approach. Anything too rigid and you will end up trying to bang square pegs into round holes, and it just won't work.

It's not just about consolidating things indiscriminately; it's about getting the balance right. Yes, your CV needs to be a good length, legible and highly presentable. However, it also needs to be relevant and powerful enough to sell your skills to the employer. In addition to this, you need to be flexible about how you include extra entries to add value to your CV.

KEYWORDS

Even if you have a good CV as a base, you may still need to make changes each time depending upon the job in question. For example, different employers look for different skills and personal traits, and you should be flexible enough to tweak your CV accordingly for each application. Saying that, some people do actually go overboard in all of this, and oversell their skills unrealistically. So when you do make additions to your CV at the very least they should be realistic, and directed at the right level for you and the job in question. One good way to do this is to look at the job specification, highlight keywords related to what the employer is looking for, and then incorporate entries based around putting relevant keywords for you into your CV. Please note the phrase '*for you*'. This is important. If the job specification mentions that the employer is looking for someone with language skills, you need to be realistic about your language ability and tell it as it is, rather than risk becoming unstuck at a later date by claiming fluent linguistic prowess in 23 different languages.

Using job specifications as a base to optimise your CV is a good technique, and most people are realistic about how they go about it. While it is not a bad thing at all to aim high, most people still have the common sense to apply only for jobs they have a realistic chance of landing. A quick glance at the job specification is usually enough to tell a potential candidate whether or not he or she is in with a shout of the job, especially if the job specification lists essential requirements (as many job specifications do).

Incorporating keywords from the job specification into your CV does achieve results, so if you don't already do this then it is something you should consider. Essentially, job specifications can be viewed as big obvious hints right from the horse's mouth as to what the employer is looking for. If you ignore job specifications and submit your application without close reference to them then this is a lazy way of applying for jobs. While job specifications are a bit of a pain for many people, for others they are a godsend, because at least a job specification gives them a handle on some of the main points they need to address in the application. Make no mistake, if used correctly job specifications are a help, not a hindrance, to job applications.

That said, you do still need to be careful how you go about things. Obviously, if you just copy and paste whole phrases from the job specification into your CV verbatim then this will come across as conspicuous or artificial. However, if you are creative enough you will be able to weave keywords naturally into your CV, and back them up with real-life, proactive examples. If you do this well then essentially you are telling the employer things that he or she wants to hear. This contributes to rousing the employer's interest and grabbing his or her attention. Of course, weaving keywords into CVs naturally is easier said than done, and there is a bit of a knack to it. But if you have a way with words then this latent ability does eventually blossom with time, practice and experience.

Let's look at the process in detail. And if you are thinking of applying for a job soon and have the job specification to hand then please fish it out now and place it alongside your CV.

The first thing to do is to read through the specification to get a better understanding of what the employer is looking for. I find it particularly useful initially to just read the specification through once or twice without actually doing anything – just taking things in. This gives you a good general overview, and sometimes it also helps you read between the lines. For example, a while ago I helped a journalist apply for a job advertised in an entertainment sector publication. His original application was very plain, rather dull and quite matter-of-fact. If I had just taken the job specification at face value then what I would have written for the client would also have been strictly professional and by-the-book. However, looking at some of the language used in the specification and reading between the lines, I could see the employer was hoping for someone with not only a sense of humour, but also the courage and ability to write in a more street-wise, thought-provoking manner. Before I wrote anything, therefore, I highlighted this observation to the client who wholeheartedly agreed and gave me the go-ahead to write in a far more hip, entertaining and risqué way than he had previously considered.

Of course, some job applications do require a more professional approach, but the above example illustrates that it sometimes pays to keep an open mind and write flexibly where necessary.

Once I have read through the job specification a couple of times to get a good overview, the next thing I do is read through it again, this time highlighting keywords and key phrases in a different colour. By keywords and key phrases I mean important things that the employer is looking for in relation to the job in question. For example, an HGV driver job specification may include keywords such as *loading*, *strapping*, *shunting*, *class 1 C + E qualified* etc.

Each job specification is different, but if you read through them carefully you can generally get a good idea of the kind of things the employer is looking for.

Hands-on session

This exercise is designed to help you think about keywords and key phrases, and to give you some hands-on practice in incorporating keywords in a CV.

The example used is based on a real job specification and a long original client CV. It is a scientific CV, and the client was targeting a particular academic job. While the job you are targeting may be completely different, the same principles apply, and you can use these techniques to improve your own job applications.

Without further ado let's get stuck in.

The first thing you need to do is read through the job specification, and then try to pick out keywords/key phrases. Make a list of these keywords and phrases on a piece of paper.

I will go and get myself a cup of coffee while I'm waiting for you to finish ...

Job specification:

Mitigation and adaptation of risks posed by global climate change are the main focus. Outstanding candidates who are experts in (but not limited to) the environment, sustainable energy/growth, planetary sustainability, water systems (quantity and quality), mineral processing, and who can make real contributions to the above priority area, are particularly encouraged to apply. Those interfacing between physical, chemical, life, computer and policy sciences are also encouraged to apply.

Our professors are scholars and teachers holding a doctorate or its professional equivalent who are widely recognised for their distinction and must have a distinguished record of achievement as evidenced by leadership in their field of expertise, publications, professional recognition, as well as a commitment to excellence in teaching.

Candidates must have a PhD degree with strong research and (graduate and undergraduate) teaching experience.

Okay. I've had my caffeine fix, biccie and brief strum on my guitar – hopefully enough time for you to have completed the exercise.

Let's now compare your list with mine. I have put the keywords in bold in the job specification below. Please note that it is not the end of the world if your keywords are different from mine, there is some degree of flexibility. The main thing to remember is that you should include key elements that the employer wants to hear.

Job specification:

Mitigation *and* **adaptation** *of* **risks** *posed by* **global climate change** *are the main focus. Outstanding candidates who are experts in (but not limited to) the* **environment, sustainable energy/growth, planetary sustainability, water systems** *(quantity and quality),* **mineral processing,** *and who can make real contributions to the above priority area, are particularly encouraged to apply. Those interfacing between physical, chemical, life, computer and policy sciences are also encouraged to apply.*

Our **professors** *are scholars and* **teachers** *holding a* **doctorate** *or its professional equivalent who are widely recognised for their distinction and must have a* **distinguished record** *of achievement as*

▶

evidenced by **leadership** in their field of **expertise, publications,** professional recognition, as well as a **commitment** to **excellence** in **teaching**.

Candidates must have a **PhD** degree with strong **research** and **(graduate and undergraduate)** teaching experience.

Once you have identified keywords you can then integrate them into the CV. One way of doing this is to create your CV first, and then add keywords and phrases afterwards. Personally, however, I find it more effective to write the whole CV with keywords in mind. If you do this it helps shape the CV as a whole, and the end result is a document that not only reads more naturally, but is also better focused. This is especially the case if you manage to weave all the keywords in naturally – this is something which is easier said than done and does take practice, but the best CV writers can do this.

In a real-life scenario I would work directly from the client's original sentences, but to make things easier for you I have already derived and refined down a few sentences from some of the client's original entries and listed these below.

I've done part of the work, now it's your turn to test your CV targeting skills by adding some keywords from the job specification into the entries below.

Time for another cup of coffee!

- … manager for leading academic institutions
- Senior lecturer across a range of …
- Successfully led a team of scientists on the implementation of …
- Conducted extensive research on atmospheric, space …

Do have a go at inserting some keywords into the above sentences before you read on. You can also try creating some new sentences of your own from scratch.

Okay, I trust you not to cheat (well, most of you anyway), so let's (naively?) assume you've all had a go and continue by looking at some of the ways in which you could have added keywords:

- Associate **professor** and scientific **research** manager for leading academic institutions

- Senior lecturer across a range of **climate change, sustainable energy and planetary sustainability** subjects

- Successfully led a team of scientists on the implementation of innovative **sustainable growth** tools

- Conducted extensive research on atmospheric, space, **water systems, mineral processing** and **environmental** energy modeling

The above is just one way of adding such keywords, there are many possible permutations. How did you do with yours? Did you include as many keywords? Do they read naturally? Are your sentences short like those above, or on the long side?

There is no one right way of adding keywords, but if what you say addresses the job specification, is relevant, reflects your actual achievements and comes across as both natural and proactive then you are on the right track. Of course, this takes a lot of thought and practice, especially if you want to include all the keywords in just one page as the best writers can do. Nevertheless, I wouldn't expect you to create a perfectly targeted high-impact CV at the first time of asking. The main thing you should take from this exercise is confidence in knowing that you can make your CV of greater interest to prospective employers. And that is a very good starting point by any stretch of the imagination.

Talking of starting – if you do have details of a position of interest that you want to target, then now is as good a time as any to get the job in your sights, draw back that mental bow of yours and let those keyword arrows rip.

Kiss of life

I fell asleep reading a dull book and dreamed I kept on reading, so I awoke from sheer boredom. HEINRICH HEINE

Looking into my crystal ball I am now going to attempt to pre-empt one of your questions.

Could it be *'So how do I make my own CV less generic and more specialist?'* by any chance?

This is certainly a question that you need to ask yourself no matter how good you think your CV is at the moment. Significantly, it is also a question we have already started to answer – just refer back to the keywords section, and the work we have just done for our old friend Joe. Do you think you could apply some of the lessons from his CV to yours?

More than likely – and there is nothing stopping you from bounding across the room this very instant to retrieve your CV from that smelly

sock drawer, pinch it by the nose, and have a go at breathing some fresh new life into it.

RULEZZZZ

Additionally (and importantly), this question of specialism isn't something that you need to ask yourself just the once, but something that you need to ask every time you go job-hunting. CVs are dynamic documents and change through time. So even if your CV was well focused a few years ago, it may not be the case now that you have added one or two extra jobs in the interim. Not only that, but people's career aspirations change through time, so now it could be entirely feasible that you are targeting not only a different job type, but a different level of job too. If this is the case then this also needs to be addressed in your CV.

I keep coming back to this matter (probably because it is extremely important), but flexibility and the ability to have a resourceful and open mind certainly help when it comes to writing your CV, and this certainly applies when it comes to optimising your CV.

Traditionalists will have you writing paragraphs about each and every job, regardless of whether they are relevant or of any interest to the employer. If you remember I asked you earlier to take out a big eraser and rub out any previous conceptions about CV writing. In that case I hope that this particular traditional CV-writing myth is well and truly erased by now. No matter what your *friend who knows all about CVs* tells you, there is no cast-iron CV-writing rule which dictates that you have to list every last detail of every last job. Moreover, if you do so there are usually more disadvantages than advantages.

So why do it? Your CV needs to be concise, pertinent and of great interest to the employer. How anyone can think the addition of lots of superfluous (usually padded out and repetitive) entries is going to do anything other than bore and deter an employer is beyond me. Referring back to the whole purpose of the CV, it is to grab the employer's attention, not send him to sleep.

Don't worry, we will discover ways of knocking those ridiculous myths into touch and keeping the employer wide awake and eager to know more throughout the following chapters.

THE GHOST OF JOB APPLICATIONS TO COME

Annual income twenty pounds, annual expenditure nineteen pounds nineteen and six, result happiness. Annual income twenty pounds, annual expenditure twenty pounds nought and six, result misery. WILKINS MICAWBER IN *DAVID COPPERFIELD* (CHARLES DICKENS)

So, we have established that part of the trick of turning generic CVs into more specialist and captivating CVs has its roots in flexibility, and the courage and common sense to blatantly ignore traditional CV-writing claptrap (as also told by quite a few modern day Dickensian recruiters I might add).

Fall into this claptrap trap at your peril. Yes, you are bound to get a slap on the back from some people with bushy sideburns, moustaches and top hats, but take heed dear sir or madam, follow this advice when you send off your application and it may just mysteriously disappear into the city fog, never to be seen again.

But let's assume you want to go down the more modern, proactive route. What next?

You can't just get rid of every single irrelevant job can you? Otherwise, according to some, the employer will wonder what you have been doing your entire career.

Well, there is no set formula for this, but as mentioned it pays to be open-minded, creative and flexible.

I'VE FINISHED, LET'S GET STARTED

This paper by its very length defends itself against the risk of being read. WINSTON CHURCHILL (WHEN HANDED A PARTICULARLY LONG MEMORANDUM)

A lot of CV writers already have an idea of what the finished article will say and look like even before they start the writing process. This is especially the case if they work to fixed formulas and rigid templates, as many CV writers do.

However, personally speaking, I never even know what I will say, let alone how long the document will be, or even how it will be formatted, until I get into the actual writing process and try various scenarios to see which one works best.

I have previously referred to CV-writing rules and myths. Funnily enough, some of the most commonly perceived rules are actually myths, but nonetheless, some of these myths are actually fundamentals (and Churchill thought Russia was enigmatic!).

Okay, let me elaborate.

If you listen to some of the bushy-sideburn brigade then your CV needs to be exactly one, or two, or three, or four pages long (depending on the law as decreed by rule 16 subsection 2.4 of the *Cast-Iron CV-Writing Bible* of whichever branch of the bushy-sideburn brigade your contact adheres to). The myth in this instance is that CVs have to be a set length. This is utter nonsense and anyone who says this has been force-fed too much 100-year-old gruel. However, scratch away at the myth and underneath the surface is something which is not only pertinent but is also pretty (no, very) important: namely, *CV length*. So while these rule-mongers may be barking up the wrong tree with their blind and rigid adherence to myths, at least they have recognised the importance of paying particular attention to a fundamental issue (and I certainly class CV length as a fundamental issue).

We will investigate and expose this and other myths in the next chapter.

5

CV writing myths

In this chapter I have listed some common CV-writing myths. Some myths are relatively harmless, while at the same time others are counterproductive, verging on the potentially dangerous. To help identify these I have continued using the traffic light system, with red obviously still at the more dangerous end of the scale.

There are a terrible lot of lies going around the world, and the worst of it is half of them are true.

WINSTON CHURCHILL

... critically you will be better placed to differentiate between CV *musts* and *myths*. You should also be far better placed to identify which *'advisers'* really do know about CVs as opposed to the many charlatans who claim to, but in reality haven't the foggiest ...

Size matters – length

As mentioned, if you listen to some people they will tell you quite categorically that CVs should be written in a particular way. However, if you listen to other people they will tell you in no uncertain terms that CVs should be written in a totally different way and include completely different things.

Not everyone can be right. So, by definition some people are definitely wrong. Or are they? Well, actually I do think that some people are wrong, but many who are wrong are in a sense right, albeit somewhat unwittingly. If this isn't confusing enough some people are also right but for the wrong reasons!

The truth of the matter is that there are not as many cast-iron rules about CV writing as people think. Indeed, there are numerous myths, and if you follow these myths rather than common sense then the quality of your CV, and ultimately your job prospects, may suffer.

If you are too rigid in your CV-writing approach you will become unstuck. Many people who take an excessively rigid approach do so because they believe in the myths, and bow to their own particular self-styled oracle rather than defer to common sense.

To elaborate, let's consider the first myth: CV *length.* Depending on who you speak to some people will tell you quite categorically that CV length should be one, or two, or three, or four pages. Again, everyone can't be right. So who is?

'I am!' I can hear all the so-called CV experts shouting in confident unison.

'It's one …' 'It's two …' 'It's three …' 'It's four …'

Regardless of what anyone tells you, the answer really depends on you, what you have done, and what you are looking to do.

Why should a school leaver have a CV which is the same length as someone who has twenty years' experience? Unless the employer has specifically requested a CV to a particular length, then the best thing for you to do is to write your CV and let it find its own natural length. If you approach this in any other way your CV risks looking artificial.

So, if in your case your work experience and qualifications are such that you can fit everything comfortably on your CV in two pages then the best length for your CV is two pages, regardless of any myth you may have heard.

In this case, the person who said two pages was right. However, as mentioned above you can be right for the wrong reason. So if you chose the correct page length, but chose it to coincide with a myth, rather than basing your decision on natural length, then you are right for the wrong reason.

There are probably more myths than there are CV-writing musts, so you just have to use your common sense. For example, if someone told you CVs should be no more than one page long and you need to use cramped text and miniscule fonts to do this then really your common sense should tell you that perhaps something isn't right.

Similarly, if you have been told that CVs should be four pages long, but do not have enough content or work experience to fill more than three pages, then common sense should tell you to stop earlier, rather than waffle on to four. Significantly, I have been told by numerous HR executives that they don't read CVs which are longer than three pages, and while this doesn't apply across the board it is certainly noteworthy and worth considering. Remember, the best CVs say more but with fewer words and really three pages should be easily enough (or even more than enough). I have written CVs for many seasoned professionals at the top of their field. These people tend to have a wealth of experience and many highly impressive achievements, certainly a lot more than Mr Average. Consequently, their CVs are often four or more pages in length to begin with. Nevertheless, personally speaking, I always end up refining their CV down to a maximum of just one or two pages. Saying that, I wouldn't rule out the possibility of a longer CV in very exceptional circumstances (for example, care home managers sometimes need longer CVs depending on the employer's criteria), so generally you need to be flexible and open-minded. However, virtually all CVs can be refined down to two pages, or better still a high-impact one-page document with a bit of thought, creativity, time and effort.

One of the reasons I consider length as a fundamental is touched upon above. First and foremost your CV needs to be enticing enough to get read. Without that, it is irrelevant whether or not you have phrased everything perfectly or have included an interests section. And while you personally may think it is great to include every last detail of every last job (and end up with a five-page CV as a result), significantly many HR executives couldn't care less what you think. With only so many hours in the day and tall piles of CVs on their desks to get through, often all they are interested in is finding someone who fits the bill. You should remember that HR executives have seen a great many CVs and will be well aware of the fact that long CVs tend to be padded out with a lot of superfluous, repetitive or irrelevant information. Significantly, many HR executives only have a set amount of time allocated to reading CVs. With this in mind you can be sure that longer CVs are less enticing to read (or even a deterrent to read) compared to better proportioned ones.

Another thing to consider is that, contrary to common perceptions, HR executives don't just sit around reading CVs all day long. They have a wide variety of other tasks and duties to perform including administration, attending meetings, working on training/workshops and much more besides. Indeed, some of the HR executives I have spoken to have told me that they allocate only a relatively small time slot in their working week to look through CVs. Moreover, frequently this time slot is disproportionate to the number of CVs received. Consequently, there has to be some give, and sometimes this results in less enticing CVs being discarded before they are even read.

With reference to padding out your CV, if you do this it also tells the employer something significant about you and your (lack of) ability to communicate in a concise and constructive manner. For some jobs this isn't such a big deal. For example, if you are a welder it probably won't be the end of the world if your CV is too long, providing you have demonstrated that you have relevant skills, qualifications and experience. However, if you are applying for jobs where communication skills are more important, such as administration, sales or marketing-related jobs, then you could come unstuck. The reason for this becomes obvious if you put yourself in the employer's shoes. Just ask yourself this: if you were going to employ a marketing professional would you engage someone who presented you with a long and padded-out CV? Or would you prefer someone with a slick, concise and more pertinent document?

Among other things, employers in sectors such as sales and marketing look for people who can sell themselves in a high-impact manner in their CV, because if they can't sell themselves they will probably struggle out there in the big bad world when it comes to promoting the company's products and services.

It is therefore no surprise that the likes of sales, marketing and communications experts frequently *specifically* ask me to write one-page

CVs for them. Not only that, but others (including HR executives, managers, directors and job seekers in all sectors) are increasingly waking up to the advantages of shorter (especially one-page) CVs. Many of these people have a lot to shout about, which is why their original CVs are often long (too long). They actually know that their CVs are too long, it's just that because they are using conventional formats/methods, and don't know how to write concisely yet proactively, they struggle to refine their CV down to the optimum length (and while I do have an open mind about CV length, I nevertheless believe that the optimum length for most people is one page).

While refining your CV down in a high-impact manner is easier said than done, this book should help you do just that, whether you think your optimum length is one page or two

The truth about lies – CV (un)truths

There are three kinds of lies: lies, damned lies, statistics ... and CV rules. BENJAMIN DISRAELI

Okay, I will own up and say that I added on the ending to the above quotation myself. See? – you should be somewhat sceptical about anything purporting to be a CV-writing must, because some so-called *'truths'* are really falsehoods masquerading as reality. Let's just assess one of these perceived *'facts'* for a moment:

Fact 507B (as decreed by East Acton bushy-sideburn branch's CV-writing bible): 'Everyone lies on their CV'

If this were true (let's start with some irony, why not?), then there would be 100 applicants for each job with the industry of Churchill, the brain of Einstein, and the business/philanthropic characteristics and achievements of Rockefeller.

There is only one problem (a lie for starters) with this theory – namely, that employers are not stupid, and a lot of people are more honest than others give them credit for.

The truth of the matter (real truth this time!) is that not everyone lies on their CV; on the contrary, many people only include entries that they can comfortably (and honestly) back up if probed at interview.

Obviously, it's up to you if you want to try to deceive the employer, but I wouldn't recommend it, and it could backfire on you big time if you attempt it.

On a somewhat related note – there is another big lie in the world of CV advice, and it revolves around certain well-dressed impostors who claim to know everything there is to know about CV writing, whereas in reality they have done no research on the subject, can't write, and wouldn't know a good CV if it bit them on the bum.

They know who they are – or rather just some of them do – ah, the deluded and should-be-eluded haughtily preaching from their lofty pin-striped pedestals ... poetic and evocative – but a recipe for disaster.

More on this subject later.

 # Poor form format

Statement 47F (as decreed by the Putney Puritans' Curriculum Vitae Guild): 'CVs need to be presented in one particular way'

By this I am referring to the fact that some people will tell you quite categorically that CVs need to be written to an exact format.

There is some truth in this lie in that CVs certainly need to be in a highly presentable format, but there is no truth in the assertion that it has to be a particular format, consisting of a predefined structure and layout.

I have seen hundreds of CV formats over the years, and while at least 80 per cent are poor in one or more respects, the rest are quite decent in the main, and probably won't hinder the applicants' chances because of the format alone. Also, any kind of layout is subjective to some degree, and just because one person tells you that a particular format is the best it doesn't necessarily mean that this is indeed the case or that everyone agrees with this view. In fact, the one absolute certainty is that not everyone will agree!

Obviously, there are some constants. For example, something which is neat, presentable and uncluttered is probably better than something which is big, bold, colourful and jam-packed from head to toe with word upon word. Saying that, beauty is in the eye of the beholder and you actually never know. The best advice is often to play it safe with something slick and professional. And while it is true that if you try to be too bold then you enter the realms of subjectivity, it is also true that you just never know the tastes of the employer at the other end. Try to be too different and the odds are probably against you, but on the other hand some long shots do end up romping home.

For example, I have heard of cases where restaurant professionals have landed jobs with CVs in a menu format. I also know of cases where design professionals have secured employment with CVs with more unusual layouts. Significantly however, the layouts in question were not bad or untidy – they were just *different*. This is highly relevant. I don't think there is anything wrong with being different as long as it is attracts and entices the employer. With this in mind the above examples don't really come into the '*long shot*' category at all, and certainly nowhere near as much as some of the CVs I have seen with huge bold pink headers, weird graphics and smiley faces.

Let me qualify that – your qualifications

... quite possibly something rather surprising about CV qualifications sections ...

As mentioned, when I write CVs I have an open mind and while I usually have a good idea what the final format will look like, I am never sure until I have tried out various scenarios to see which one works best. For example, pretty much all my CVs have *profile, work experience* and *skills* sections, but not all of them have an *interests* or even a *qualifications* section.

Some of you (including many CV writers) may be surprised to hear this. However, there is always method in my madness, and always a very good reason for things. For instance, as previously said, I sometimes deliberately exclude qualifications. Yes, admittedly this is somewhat unconventional, but sometimes it pays to be a bit creative especially if it is advantageous, as it is in some cases.

There is no CV-writing rule which says you have to include every last qualification. Sometimes it is disadvantageous to do so, which is why it is sometimes wise to refrain from convention rather than just blindly following this myth.

You need to remember that CV writing is akin to a delicate balancing act. If you include everything the document just grows in length, and loses focus, impact and direction. You have to be far cuter than just adding everything willy-nilly. For the best results you also have to weigh up all the pros and cons of what to include and what to exclude, and prioritise them according to what is more fundamental.

One of the reasons why it is sometimes advantageous to exclude qualifications relates to the need to keep your CV relevant and a good length. So, for example, if you are targeting a chief accountant post it may be worth mentioning your accounting degree but it will probably be completely redundant to mention your GCSE in woodwork. This may seem like common sense, but a surprising number of people include minor, irrelevant qualifications which are superseded by far better and infinitely more pertinent ones. Worse still, a lot of people fall into the trap of including every single grade of every certificate they have ever taken. Again, this is not necessary at all, and personally I wouldn't include grades unless they are relevant and impressive.

Sometimes I omit the qualifications section altogether, not just refine it. Usually when I do this it has less to do with factors such as space constraints and more to do with considering the competition and selling the candidate's plus points.

For example, if someone is targeting a senior business development manager job but only has 'A' levels in English Literature and History I would consider excluding the whole qualifications section.

You need to think about the competition. Managerial jobs are extremely competitive, and there is no doubt whatsoever that candidates for such jobs will be competing against people with degrees, MBAs, and professional management certification. Paradoxically, if you include your perfectly decent English Literature and History 'A' level qualifications, rather than impressing the employer it could just draw attention to the fact that you do not possess the same academic credentials as some of your competitors.

If the candidate possessed good professional qualifications or certification then I would consider replacing the 'qualifications' section with a different one along the lines of perhaps 'professional qualifications' or 'selected professional training'. However, if the candidate did not possess such credentials then I would consider omitting the qualifications section altogether.

Sometimes it pays to be a bit creative, and this involves not just working out what it is best to include, but also deciding what it is best to omit.

What about you?

Now that you've learned some things you possibly didn't know before let's re-examine your qualifications section. Does it get top marks at the first time of asking? Or do you need a resit?

Off the mark – grades

I was thrown out of college for cheating on the metaphysics exam; I looked into the soul of the boy sitting next to me. WOODY ALLEN

On the subject of qualifications I have been asked many times whether or not to include qualification grades on CVs. Again this is something which certain rule-mongers proclaim is absolutely necessary, but in reality it is nothing of the sort and is merely an artificially contrived myth.

As with many other CV-writing myths, if you apply even an ounce of common sense to the equation then the myth is exposed for what it is: namely, naive and bad advice if carried out indiscriminately to the letter. As ever, a more logical and flexible approach is preferable.

You need to remember that your CV isn't the Domesday Book, and its purpose isn't to chronicle every small step and every minute detail of your work and life history. The ultimate purpose of your CV is to entice the employer enough to offer you an interview. The best way to do this is to accentuate your positives, not over-elaborate or highlight negatives.

Yes, I do realise that some recruiters tell candidates to include even poor qualification grades on their CVs, and like polite sheep some candidates baaa down to them and comply. However, the job market isn't a particularly level playing field, and just because you dutifully include poor grades on your CV this doesn't necessarily mean that your competitors will follow suit. Some will undoubtedly be cuter than you and use a bit of creative licence to work their qualifications section to their advantage.

Hands-on session

Just a quickie mini practical session for you to keep the old brain cells ticking over (okay, and also to check you are listening!).

Let's imagine that your qualifications section looks like this:

- GCSE English (C) – 1982
- GCSE Art (C) – 1982
- GCSE French (D) – 1982
- GCSE Physics (C) – 1982
- GCSE Mathematics (C) – 1982
- GCSE Metal work (C) – 1982
- GCSE History (C) – 1982
- GCSE Geography (C) – 1982
- A-level English (E) – 1984
- A-level History (E) – 1984
- A-level Geography (F) – 1984

So does yours look anything like that?

Whether it does or not, either way the list is taking up a lot of space, and isn't particularly impressive, especially as a competitor with exactly the same exams/grades might display their qualifications in a more effective manner.

Can you think of a way of doing this more succinctly?

If nothing strikes you immediately then don't worry. Just get up and put the kettle on. You can consider potential options while the water is boiling.

A judge is a law student who marks his own examination papers. H.L. MENCKEN

Well now that you are suitably physically and mentally refreshed, how about this possibility?

- 7 O-levels including English and Mathematics and 2 A-levels (1982 to 1984)

You could be forgiven for thinking that the first list is better, because at the very least there is more of it, and it is more detailed. However, whenever you write your CV you shouldn't just write everything down without any thought, care and attention. Instead, at each and every stage you need to consider the employer, your competitors, and how best to highlight your positives rather than negatives.

In the above example the second qualifications section would probably be more productive than the first one. The first qualifications section takes up a lot of vital vertical space to say very little (space which could be far better used selling relevant skills). Additionally, not only does the first example show that the candidate failed exams, but it also shows that the candidate didn't achieve particularly impressive GCSE grades. This is significant because employers are not stupid, and many employers are of a certain age where exams were arguably tougher in their day and they are unlikely to be impressed by someone who just scraped through GCSEs.

The first example is actually an illustration of someone trying to be too clever for their own good, and replacing O-levels with GCSEs (which didn't even exist in the early 1980s).

A lot of people do themselves a disservice by replacing O-levels with GCSEs, or by not putting dates on A-levels which were gained at a time when A-levels were perceived as far harder to pass. This concept of perception is important. In a job/career context, it doesn't really matter what educators, government ministers, the media or even you and I think. The main thing is what employers think. And judging by conversations I have had with employers and HR executives, it appears that GCSEs and modern A-levels are less favourably perceived than O-levels and less recent A-levels; not only that but the very fact that someone has good O-levels is frequently an indicator of age and experience – which is no bad thing. It is therefore worth bearing this in mind when you write your qualifications section.

A structured approach – format

Reason has always existed, but not always in a reasonable form. KARL MARX

… the way you present your information is extremely important, and there is more to it than meets the eye. This section gives you food for thought and something to chew on … bon appétit!

In a previous section, I mentioned the fact that some CV formats probably won't hinder the applicants' chances because of the format alone.

I think I should elaborate here.

While some CV formats are quite reasonable on the surface, and look fairly presentable, it is not insignificant that some formats are better than others (and on different levels). The significance is heightened by the fact that often there is just one successful candidate per job on offer. Consequently, your CV needs to be far better than just reasonable: it needs to stand out over and above the competition.

When most people consider format, they tend to think in terms of just what it looks like. However, as with pretty much every aspect of CV writing, there is more to it than meets the eye. It is rather like owning a wedding car hire company. You want your cars to stand out from the crowd, and turn heads. So they need to be sleek, elegant and suitably sized. In addition to this, the insides need to be swish, plush and sophisticated. If this isn't enough, you also need to ensure the motor is in tiptop condition if you are to ferry your clients to church in time on their special day.

CV writing isn't a million miles away from this analogy. Obviously, any CV worth its salt needs to be a good length and highly presentable on the surface, but more than this, once you get inside it that too needs to be neat, pertinent, and highly legible. On top of this, the whole thing needs not only the right parts and structure, but these also need weaving together naturally like a well-oiled machine if your CV is to get you to your destination (in this case an interview room).

Just as there are different varieties of great wedding cars, there are equally a number of CV formats which do the job well enough. When it comes to doing the job *really well*, however, the drop-out rate does go up several notches because CV formats which can do this are fewer and farther between.

Part of the reason why this is so tricky relates to the dynamics of CV writing. The best formats cover all the important things, but do so in a stylish, highly legible and sufficiently concise manner. This is easier said than done. Indeed, many formats fall down at this hurdle because their dynamics are such that although they can pull most of the pieces of the jigsaw together, they find it impossible to do *all* of the above without compromising on some aspects such as length, legibility or presentation.

Little wonder therefore that many people end up pulling their hair out trying to fit their career neatly into their apparently presentable but patently flawed CV templates. Sometimes it is akin to trying to stuff a whole filing cabinet worth of pristine documents into a sleek and petite attaché case. This is an impossible task that a great many people attempt and inevitably fail, much to their frustration, distress and despair. Just as some of nature's most beautiful creatures are also among the most deadly, some CV formats are pretty enough to entice people to use them, but sufficiently flawed to kill their chances of interview stone dead. Really some templates and formats should come with a hazard warning!

Yes, the format you use needs to be highly presentable and attractive, but it also needs to be structured well enough to allow you to sell your message in a clear, sharp manner without exceeding the optimum length or compromising on legibility. If the format you are using does not allow you to do this then that is an indication that there is something wrong.

(Un)kind candid camera – photographs

Men are not prisoners of fate, but only prisoners of their own minds. FRANKLIN D. ROOSEVELT

Rule 202-c (as decreed by Mayfair's all-star governor's top hat CV-Writing Lodge): 'CVs need to include photographs'

Adding photographs on CVs is generally not done in the UK, the USA and many countries. However, it is more prevalent in some other countries. A good general rule is if the employer does not ask for a photograph then do not include one.

There are some exceptions to this. For example, if you are an actor or a model then adding photographs is often expected. Additionally, sometimes it may be advantageous to include a photograph. If you are applying for a job in a sector such as the service industry where presentation is often important and you are very photogenic, then it may actually help your application if you include a photograph. Saying that, if you do this you are entering the realms of subjectivity so be careful. I have seen a great many CVs which include photographs and I strongly suspect that the inclusion of a photograph for many of these people is actually a deterrent to employment rather than an aid. Indeed, some applicants look more like convicts or rabbits trapped in headlights than professionals looking for a job.

The devil's in the detail – personal information

Man's main task in life is to give birth to himself, to become what he potentially is.

ERICH FROMM

Rules 16, 17B, 21F and 64G (as decreed by Shepherd Bush Bushies CV fraternity): 'CVs need to include date of birth, gender, marital status and nationality'

There is a grey area around the inclusion of date of birth, marital status and nationality in CVs. Again, these are things which some people will tell you quite categorically need to be included, and others will tell you quite categorically need to be omitted. Again, my preference is for a more common-sense approach along the lines of 'include them if they are advantageous or useful, and exclude them if they are not'.

As far as gender and marital status is concerned, personally speaking I do not normally include these. The reason has nothing to do with rules 17B and 21F, but more to do with pragmatism: the plain fact is that they are not strictly necessary and if you want to include them this takes up valuable space that can be better used to include something far more proactive, important and relevant. That said, if you feel that the employer is, for example, particularly seeking someone who is single, and you are indeed single, then in such cases it could be advantageous to include it. An instance might be if you were applying for a job as a Club 18–30 representative then it may be advantageous to state that you are single.

Nationality and date of birth (or just age if you are uncomfortable with including your date of birth) are a bit different, and I tend to include them in most instances.

'Oh, you shouldn't do that!' I hear some of the Shepherd Bush Bushies bleat – *'Anti-discrimination laws and all that.'* Nevertheless, regardless of what some of my hirsute peers rigidly advocate, my own personal opinion is that there is a good case for inclusion, for the following reasons.

First, these are things that employers want to know anyway – regardless of anti-discrimination guidelines, if an employer is a fully-fledged xenophobe or ageist then he or she will not employ the candidate anyway even if they get to interview. If this is the case why go through all the hassle of correspondence, phone calls, travelling, time and expense of attending interviews just to prolong the inevitable? To my mind, it is better to be honest and upfront right from the outset. That way there is no cat-and-mouse play, false hope or additional disappointment.

Secondly (and this is something that I have noticed that many recruiters fail to realise), despite the fact that no one is obliged to add their age or nationality on a CV sometimes it is *advantageous* to do so. This is highly significant and it always amazes me when I hear of a recruiter advising someone to exclude their age on the basis of blind adherence to their perception of anti-discrimination guidelines rather than lucid intelligence and common sense. For example, if you are a 36-year-old British project manager and are applying for a project management job in the UK then you are a good age and nationality for the job in question. In which case why not mention it? To me it makes sense to do just that. Yes, you may get some finger pointing and a few *'tuts!'* from the Shepherd's Bush Bushies, but so what if you get the job?

Golden (and golden oldie) ages

Old age is not so bad when you consider the alternatives. MAURICE CHEVALIER

On the subject of age I have heard it said that there are *'golden ages'* for employment (commonly 30–35 for women and 35–40 for men) and this sounds about right for a lot of jobs. Nevertheless, it should be remembered that each job is different and consequently there is no such thing as a hard and fast *'golden age'*. Really it varies depending upon the job in question. For example, the *'golden age'* for graduate jobs could be 21, whereas the *'golden age'* for CEO jobs could be 47. Even then it is really all down to the employer and what he or she is looking for. The main thing to remember is that, regardless of what anyone tells you, sometimes it can most definitely be advantageous to include your age on a CV.

Again on the subject of age, many older job seekers hesitate to put their age on their CV because they fear that their age could count against them. While I can certainly understand and appreciate this, it is worth mentioning that some employers do positively discriminate *towards* older candidates, or people from ethnic backgrounds (even though this is supposed to be illegal). Positive discrimination can occur for genuine reasons including the appreciation of the maturity of older candidates, as well as for less pragmatic reasons including the maintenance of internal anti-discrimination quotas (even though there is no actual legislation for specific quotas). Either way, it is yet another reason for including such details on your CV.

Gender(eering)

Nobody will ever win the battle of the sexes. There's just too much fraternising with the enemy. HENRY KISSINGER

Going back to gender: if you are female and feel that your gender works against you in your job sector because it is male-dominated then you may be tempted to omit gender from your CV, especially if you have a unisex name such as Kim, Chris etc. This is understandable because some employers do discriminate against females. Nevertheless, even in male-dominated sectors some employers recognise the benefits of employing females. Indeed, research has shown that the most effective teams are ones with a good balance of age, gender, skills and backgrounds. So if you are a woman in a male-dominated arena, then this may not be such a hindrance as at first appears. And in some cases highlighting your sex on your CV may actually work to your advantage.

Moreover, while it is largely illegal, and they are not generally encouraged to do so, employers do sometimes *positively* discriminate on the basis of age, race, gender and disability. And employers do sometimes specifically word and strategically place advertisements with the deliberate intention of recruiting a particular under-represented group or type of person. So if you read an advertisement for an engineering job in a women's magazine that is probably an indication that the company in question is positively discriminating women.

I say 'largely' illegal, because there are exceptions, and it's a bit of a minefield. I'm not a lawyer, and don't claim to be (so this doesn't constitute legal advice), but in the course of my research for this book I actually had some interesting conversations with representatives from the Equality and Human Rights Commission. Initially I enquired about anti-discriminatory legislation, but ended up discussing a wider range of equality in the workplace issues. Some of this related to issues outside the scope of this book, but some of it is certainly relevant here and I have included references where appropriate.

For example, if your circumstances are such that you feel you could take advantage of positive discrimination then you would probably be better off applying to larger companies, and especially public organisations and institutions. Public sector organisations actually have a *duty* to have a representative mix of the population, to promote equality of opportunity, and work towards the elimination of discrimination on the basis of race, age, gender or disability. Despite common perception, private sector companies do not have the same duty, although many larger companies take it upon themselves to set their own targets to redress the equality balance in their own organisations.

Pride and prejudice – names

I cannot tell what the dickens his name is. MRS PAGE IN *THE MERRY WIVES OF WINDSOR*, III, II, 19 (WILLIAM SHAKESPEARE)

On the subject of discriminatory (and xenophobic) employers: one option open to you if you have a foreign-sounding name and are applying for jobs in the UK is to Anglicise it, or to shorten your first name to something a bit more in line with the English palate.

Here's an example why: a gentleman of Pakistani origin recently asked me whether or not he should change his name in his job applications for senior administration posts in public schools. His reasoning was that he had good qualifications and experience but had received several rejections. To his mind the rejections were motivated by his ethnic origin rather than his ability to do the job. To counter this he was seriously considering the possibility of using a name such as 'Mr Jones' on all his subsequent applications; and he asked for my opinion.

As part of my reply I said this:

Should you change your name?

As I can see it is a bit of a catch-22. Yes, you could Anglicise your name, and you may even get more interviews because of it. However, if an institution discriminates on the basis of ethnicity they will do it regardless of whether it is at the application stage or the interview stage. Yes, at least you may get a chance to impress and change someone's mind at interview. However, some interviewers may feel tricked if they expect a 'Mr Jones' but someone else turns up. In such cases changing your name could be completely counterproductive, and you could effectively lose a job you would otherwise have had on the basis of your perceived deception.

As a matter of fact, I also spoke to some HR executives about this. Every single one assured me in no uncertain terms that they personally would not discount anyone on the basis of ethnicity, and I do believe the people I spoke to. While I cannot speak for the selection committee of the public schools in question, looking at this gentleman's experience it was clear that although he did have significant experience, and he did have a degree, his experience was relatively short (around five years), and his degree was decent but in an unrelated discipline and with a pretty average grade. Given this information it is perfectly conceivable that the reason he was rejected had nothing to do with ethnicity, but more to do with the possibility that there were more suitable candidates for the jobs.

I don't doubt that discrimination does go on sometimes, and in a variety of forms, but I also feel that some people do underestimate the level of the competition for good jobs. Some people who think they have been discriminated against may have missed out purely and simply because there was a better candidate for the job.

Great expectations – salary

The wages of sin are death, but by the time taxes are taken out, it's just sort of a tired feeling. PAULA POUNDSTONE

... hopefully this section will save you quite a tidy sum in the long run!

Rule 82 subsection J (as decreed by the Shaftesbury Sideburn Scribblers): 'CVs should include current salary and salary aspirations'

A lot of people include their current salary and salary expectations on their CV. Again, the necessity to include salary details is a complete myth.

Personally speaking, I never include salary details in CVs, and again the basis for this has its roots in simple common sense.

If you look at the pros and cons of including a salary, the cons column will be bursting at the seams, like an overcrowded Wormwood Scrubs. The pros column, on the other hand, will be feeling rather lonely in comparison as it looks through the bars of solitary confinement at the rioters scaling the exercise-yard walls. Indeed, the only possible advantage of including salary details, as far as I can see, is an advantage for the employer, not you. So if you want to hand over the advantage to the employer, rather than retain it for yourself, then by all means include salary details. On the other hand, if you prefer to gain the upper hand yourself then you may prefer to read on ...

One reason for exclusion again relates to CV length and the need to make the optimum use of available space. However, there are significant other reasons for excluding salary details. Yes, advertising a low salary may grab the employer's attention, especially if you clearly state that you are willing to work a 16-hour day for the princely sum of £1.75. But do you really want to do that? Certainly most people want the going rate and a fair wage for a fair day's work. Employers already know and accept this. If you mention a particularly low wage on your CV then this could work in two ways. First, the employer could take the bait and pay you peanuts, or on the other side of the coin the low wage could arouse suspicion and the employer may instead ask himself or herself just why you are on such a low wage if you are as good as you say. There is contradiction in such scenarios, and this is not wasted on employers.

At the other extreme, if you pitch your salary too high then the risk is that it will simply alienate the employer, and render his or her interest stone dead in one fell swoop. Even if you pitch your salary at pretty much the right level the question remains 'Is this really doing anything for you?' To my mind it is just taking up valuable space saying something which is unnecessary. It isn't selling your skills, it isn't highlighting extra benefits you bring to the table, and it isn't adding value to your CV. This being so, it raises the question – why include it?

Another significant point to consider is your negotiating position. Say, for example, your CV has the desired effect, and you actually land an interview. If the interviewer has the authority to offer up to £30,000 in salary, and you have already stated on your CV that you are willing to accept £18,000, how much do you think the salary will be if you are offered the job? Almost certainly a lot less than if you hadn't included salary details on your CV in the first place.

Remember that sometimes employers are just as open to negotiation on salaries as you are, often more so in fact. If you tell the employer how much you are willing to accept before you even walk through the door that is akin to playing poker with your cards face up on the table. This is all well and good if salary is not that important to you, and you are willing to accept a lower rate of pay. And, make no mistake, a lot of big businesses will try to get away with paying you as little as possible if they can. If, on the other hand, you feel that your labour has a certain worth, and you want to achieve this value, then you are better off playing your cards closer to your chest. If you are the right person for the job, and you impress at interview, there is a distinct possibility that the employer will negotiate upwards rather than downwards if you play your cards right.

To whom it may concern – references

I have opinions of my own – strong opinions – but I don't always agree with them. GEORGE BUSH

Rule 66.1 (as listed in the Moustachioed Muswell Hillbillies CV manual): 'CVs should include references'

The absolute necessity to include references on your CV is another CV-writing myth, and while there are a great many people who include the names and addresses of referees on their CV, there are probably even more people who do not. Out of these some make no mention whatsoever to references, while others say something along the lines of *'references available upon request'*.

Obviously opinion is divided. Personally speaking, I do not think that there is a sensible case for inclusion of full references; all this does is take up valuable space to say something which is of little interest to the employer at this initial stage. At this early stage most employers are more concerned about whittling down the applicants to a good shortlist. If their interest is aroused they would just ask for references later if required.

Most people who include references do not think about the consequences of their actions. For example, I have lost count of the CVs I have seen where the CV length exceeds the optimum length just because the candidate has used up half a dozen extra lines adding references. As mentioned previously, CV length is extremely important, and if you exceed the optimum length one drastic consequence is that you run the risk of your CV not even being read by the employer. As far as job applications go, this is about as serious as it gets. If your CV isn't enticing enough to read, your prospects of landing a good job are as remote as a Navy recruiting office opening up in Switzerland.

My own preference as far as references are concerned is to have a section at the end saying *'references available upon request'*. While strictly speaking even this is not necessary, it usually takes up only a small amount of space, plus it rounds off the CV nicely and adds to its balance. In actual terms of added value its contribution isn't particularly tangible. However, if space allows I do like to add this, because I feel it does still make an intangible yet positive contribution. Please note: *'if space allows'*. Again you need to weigh up your priorities, and if the inclusion of a *'references available upon request'* means that something more fundamental will need to be sacrificed then the inclusion doesn't make sense. Fundamentals should always take preference.

As a bit of an aside: when you appoint your referees you would do well to keep them up to date with your career achievements. I speak from experience here. It was a long time ago now, but after getting right down to the final stage I lost out on one job I applied for simply because the referee I had appointed wasn't completely au fait with the facts about all my previous work experience. When it came to filling in the form, as a very honest person my referee said that I didn't have relevant work experience in a particular area. In fact, this wasn't the case and in reality I had quite a bit of hands-on experience in the area in question. I thought my referee knew about this, but apparently he didn't, and I arguably lost out on this good job because of a lack of communication.

Hobby horses (for courses) – interests

My interest is in the future because I'm going to spend the rest of my life there. CHARLES F. KETTERING

Rule 46C (as listed in the Wimbledon Whiskers Writers Club AGM minutes): 'CVs should include an interests section'

I think interests is one of those sections which is worth including if it adds real value or if space allows, but which isn't strictly necessary and can be sacrificed if other more fundamental entries take precedence.

It is worth pointing out that sometimes it is counterproductive to include your interests, especially if they could potentially deter the employer in any way. For example, the inclusion of dangerous sports may not endear the employer to you. Similarly, you should bear in mind that some interests are perceived differently by different people, and some more negatively than others depending on the eye of the beholder. I have seen plenty of CVs which mention affiliations to political or religious groups. This is all well and good if the employer shares your enthusiasm. However, this is far from certain, and if there is a conflict of interest it could be enough to sway the employer's enthusiasm for your application.

If you are going to include interests at least make them safe and positive. By this I mean paying particular attention to including activities which could display you in a positive light. For example, interests which show that you are active, sociable and responsible are usually good bets as long as you don't overdo it. So while it is often a good idea to include entries such as *sports* and *keep fit,* it is probably best to avoid over-elaborating and breaking this down to *deep sea diving, parachuting and rock climbing*.

Some people include interest sections regardless, whereas, as mentioned, I tend to do so only if it adds value and/or space allows. If you want to include interests but haven't scaled Mount Everest or are not captain of the GB women's squash team in your spare time, then don't worry, the employer is unlikely to think that you are dull just because you list instead sewing, cooking and socialising. While outstanding achievements are good to show off if you have them, they are not the be all and end all. Besides, the main things employers look for in this section are usually just snippets to get a bit more of an idea about you as a person; and someone who can sew, cook and get on with people is no bad thing. Besides, if the employer is a fellow thimble-thumbed gourmet chatterbox who doesn't give a stuff about playing squash then you could be in business.

But what if I don't include any interests at all?

Again, the employer is hardly going to think you bore for Britain just because you don't include interests. In fact, most employers won't even notice the section isn't there, and they are not going to give your application any less weight in its absence. But if you have excluded your interests section because of space constraints, and would like to include it, then there is one way of including it without it eating too much into the space for your all-important achievements section, and that is by writing your interests in a very space-efficient manner. I tend to include them neatly, but on just one line. And you can do the same. We will learn more about writing concisely later in this book.

There we go – happy now?

Stating the obvious – objectives

The obscure we see eventually. The completely obvious, it seems, takes longer. EDWARD R. MURROW

Rule 126C (as listed in the Bermondsey Beards CV rulebook): 'CVs should include an objectives section'

Objectives sections are usually more common in American résumés than British and European CVs. There is certainly no CV-writing rule which states that you definitely need to include them, and judging by the amount of CVs I receive in the UK, most British people do not. Nevertheless, some people do still include them, either alongside or instead of a profile section.

Typically, objectives sections are short statements (usually between one and three lines) which almost invariably state the obvious in a frequently vague and oblique manner such as: *'seeking employment within sales for a leading organisation'*.

I have read a great many objectives over the years, and I don't think I recall ever reading one single objectives section which was particularly interesting, let alone inspirational or anything other than mind-numbingly stale.

In fact, objectives sections always strike me as blindingly obvious. I have never yet seen one which actually adds true value to a CV and, for the life of me, I can't see why anyone would want to include one. I strongly suspect that the only reason people do is because someone somewhere told them they had to, or that a bruiser from the bushy-sideburn brigade threatened them with a cauliflower ear if they didn't. Now and again I've also heard recruiters advocating inclusion of objectives. My natural response to this is to ask why. I am still waiting for a sensible answer from any of them. As far as I can tell, people who include objectives do so not for reasons of logic or common sense, but primarily just to conform robotically to an outdated myth.

More significantly, I don't think I've ever read a single objectives section which has told the employer something he or she either didn't already know or couldn't infer from the application. This being so it raises the question *'What is the point?'* If you are a large company advertising a sales job then it stands to reason that the people who apply for the post will be looking for a sales job with a large company. Let's face it, if they replied to your salesperson advertisement they are unlikely to be looking to be engaged as an astronaut!

Another point worth mentioning is that if you state in your objectives that you are looking to work for 'a large organisation' or 'a leading company' (which many people stipulate), yet nevertheless send your application out to typical small or medium companies (which many people stating such objectives do) then SME (small and medium enterprise) employers can be forgiven for immediately feeling rather insulted after reading at the top of your CV that you are not really looking to work for them but rather larger companies. Nevertheless, in spite of this anomaly you are still sending them an application anyway, presumably as a stop-gap until something better comes along.

Not surprisingly, some of these applications go straight in the bin!

I've seen recruiters add generic objectives sections like this to CVs and then encourage candidates to apply for positions which just don't fit with the career objective. I do wonder sometimes who is the most guilty: the recruiters who should know better, or the candidates who don't think to question such discrepancies?

People who preach about the wonders of all CV myths (not just objectives sections) often do so out of an unwavering obedience to their all-powerful, unquestionable myth god.

Significantly (and this is lost on a great many myth preachers) if you do want to tell the employer that you are looking for a sales job with a progressive company, and also elaborate further on your career aspirations, then there is a better place to mention all this anyway: namely, the cover letter (see Chapter 9).

Traits that grate
– personality

Two Andy Gorams
There's only two Andy Gorams

FAN'S FOOTBALL CHANTS LIGHT-HEARTEDLY AIMED AT GOALKEEPER ANDY GORAM AFTER MEDIA REPORTS THAT THE SCOTTISH GOALKEEPER SUFFERED FROM A MILD FORM OF SCHIZOPHRENIA

Rule 34b (according to the Kilburn Killjoys Career Curtail Council minutes): 'CVs need to reflect your personality'

Now and again you hear someone mention something along the lines that their CV needs to *reflect their personality*, as if this is an actual cast-iron requirement of a CV – which of course it isn't.

Yes, employers are interested in you and not just what jobs you have done or what training courses you have completed. However, there is no requirement to dissect, analyse and disseminate the latest volume of the inner workings of your psyche.

Sometimes it can even be counterproductive to go into too much detail about personality. For example, if you are a bubbly, cheerful, party animal who is applying for finance jobs then even though such traits would be great on an 18–30 Club representative application form, they may not go down too well on an accountant CV.

What some people surprisingly don't realise is that quite often the employer will give applicants an indication of the kind of personal traits they are looking for in the job specification. You are far better off addressing the job specification, and telling the employer what they want to hear, rather than just trying to bulldoze them into hearing what you want to tell them. It is a distinct and important difference.

I have tried suggesting such things to those candidates with fixed ideas; most are receptive and see the sense, but some just ignore me and include additional personal traits which don't really match the job specification. This of course is their right. At the same time I'm not quite sure what career they could pursue with a profile along the lines of '*A stubborn, blinkered know-it-all with cloth ears and a penchant for serial rejection*', unless they perhaps want to follow in the footsteps of some of the less receptive and less business-savvy applicants on *Dragons' Den*.

Out of (job) order

Half our life is spent trying to find something to do with the time we have rushed through life trying to save.
WILL ROGERS

… why some common advice is uncommonly cobblers

Rule 56 (according to the Dartford Dickensians Society): 'CVs should include all jobs and job roles in strict chronological order and include all dates'

If you've ever had the misfortune of having CV advice (read *hogwash*) given to you from one of the many self-appointed lesser recruiter oracles out there then this next section could be of particular relevance to you, so get your CV out, put on your specs, and listen up.

The myth that you need to include all jobs, job roles and achievements in strict chronological order together with dates is arguably one of the biggest contributors of all to shoddy CVs and failed job applications. Ironically, some of the loudest preachers of this myth are certain recruiters who quite frankly should know better. Obviously, this is a bit of a generalisation, and many recruiters are more far-sighted. However, some do seem stuck in the dark ages, and for no apparent reason.

I keep coming back to this but surely it is better to listen to common sense rather than artificial laws which are bandied about by self-appointed aficionados who can't even explain the benefits of their own advice when confronted (several clients have told me that they had asked recruiters to explain certain *recommendations* which flew in the face of common sense, and the recruiters in question were unable to do so – proof really that some advice is just dispensed willy-nilly with no thought, rhyme or reason).

Regardless of what certain myth-mongers say, there is no absolute obligation to include every job role and every last detail of every last job, let alone in strict chronological order. A great many winning job applications succeed where they would have otherwise failed had they adhered to the myth. Yes, employers are interested in your work history, and conventionally most people do list this in reverse chronological order (as I tend to do too). However, at the end of the day when employers read your CV they are more interested in discovering what you can do for them rather than fussing over minor ordering details. As mentioned previously, employers are very busy people, by and large when they look at CVs their immediate question is more along the lines of *'What can this person do for me?'* not *'Is the chronology absolutely ticketyboo?'*

I have come to the conclusion that my subjective account of my motivation is largely mythical on almost all occasions. I don't know why I do things. J.B.S. HALDANE

I regularly review applications from potential CV writers, and when browsing candidate CVs with my employer's hat on I can honestly say that I barely pay a second glance to dates and ordering of work entries. The main thing I usually have in mind is the question of whether or not the applicant has the potential to do the job well. And to ascertain this it is often a straightforward matter of looking at the big, obvious things rather than being distracted by formatting methodology. Significantly, if I am ever distracted or put off by anything it is CVs which are too long and padded out, rather than anything so trivial as ordering.

That said, even though most people's idea of ordering is largely based on a falsehood rather than fact, I would still generally recommend listing achievements in reverse chronological order, because, although there are some exceptions, it usually reads more logically, and if it is done right it helps set and build up the scene to impress. So while the first concept of ordering does tend to conform to the myth (albeit for the wrong reason), the second notion that employers need to see each and every job, and see each one in detail and separated out, is complete nonsense, and is just another artificially contrived tale.

Myth-mongers who rigidly bandy such inane legends about, are to my mind, guilty of irresponsibility. Paradoxically, the end result is often worse not better for the person they are supposed to be helping. Yes, admittedly sometimes it is a good idea to include, and separate out, all jobs. Indeed, I often do this myself if it is advantageous to do so. However, in order to achieve the best results and attract and maintain the employer's interest you need to be open-minded and flexible enough to take a wider perspective and be a bit more creative if need be.

For example, if you are a young retail professional, having worked for two different companies with no career breaks, then it makes perfect sense to list all your work experience in reverse chronological order.

However, wind forward 20 years and five multi-sector jobs later then the scenario changes somewhat. Whereas initially a conventional CV with each job separated out chronologically seemed the natural choice, now if the same methodology was again applied the resultant CV would almost certainly be very long (too long). It would also be somewhat confusing, covering multiple sectors and probably sending out mixed messages. Now do you get the picture? In cases like this, it not only pays to take a more flexible approach but it is pretty much essential to do so if you want to avoid a CV which is too long, confused and unfocused.

Bizarrely enough, some recruiters and so-called experts fail to see the wisdom in this, and instead cling tightly to the myth, like a proud and stubborn old captain clutching the wheel of a sinking ship as it disappears without trace into the blue, much like the CVs of the job seekers they are purportedly *advising*.

Brief aside for some tips ...

 ### FLEXING YOUR FLEXIBILITY

So how can you be flexible? And what can you do to help someone with many jobs and even a multi-sector career achieve a more focused and better-length CV?

Well, one thing you can't do is achieve this by rigidly adhering to the myth. In cases like this you need to be more inventive. Obviously, each CV is different, and each one throws up different scenarios. And there is no set formula. The best way forward for one person may involve just removing a reference to the last job, whereas for someone else the best way forward may involve something more radical such as consolidating certain jobs and dates into one entry.

Additionally, it is often a good idea to be open-minded enough to the possibility of adopting different approaches for the same person at different points in their career. Referring back to the person who started out in retail above, as mentioned at the onset of his career a traditional chronological CV may be best. Two multi-sector jobs later the best way forward could involve combining the retail jobs into one entry in order to save space and maintain optimum length. Five multi-sector jobs later and some radical changes would probably be necessary. In such cases you should take a step back, evaluate your (fresh) career goals, and then work out what new message and direction your CV needs to take in order to achieve your target, because if things have changed then what worked with your previous applications probably won't work the next time. Time, paths, circumstances, experiences and targets move on – and so must your CV if it is to keep up.

Quite paradoxically, the longer and more complex the career path, the more attractive a shorter and simpler CV solution becomes.

Significantly, many people have trouble seeing this for themselves. This is quite natural and understandable, because if you write your own CV it is harder to take a step back, and look at things from a wider perspective. A lot of people just can't see the wood for the trees, which is why many people end up making an already complicated CV even more complicated.

Sometimes, as in other areas of work or life, it takes someone to look in from the outside to get to the heart of the matter.

As mentioned, each CV is different, and you need to come at each one from a fresh perspective and potentially different angle in order to find the best way forward for the person in question. There are no set formulas. You really have to use your common sense, test out the options, and choose the right scenario for you and your circumstances and career aspirations.

The above information should at least help convince you that strict chronological CVs with separated-out jobs can sometimes do your career aspirations more harm than good, and should also give you some ideas on what you can do to give you a better chance of impressing employers. You probably already know by now that there is an awful lot more to CV writing than meets the eye, and if I went into each scenario in fine detail then the length of this book would also spiral out of control. However, I have already introduced you to a couple of excellent popular techniques which will help you proactively manage important CV fundamentals including length, message and focus. I will elaborate further on these elsewhere in this book, but, before we return to discover yet more CV-writing myths, here are some more useful tips for you:

- If your CV is more than two pages in length, it's probably too long.

- If your CV doesn't scream out (and fast) that you are an expert in the job you are targeting then that is something you need to address.

- If you sound like a jack of all trades rather than a specialist (in the job you are targeting) then your CV needs to be re-focused.

- If your CV is hard going when you read it, then that is a clear signal something is wrong.

- If in doubt, get a second opinion (and preferably a professional one from a trusted source – you can even send it to me if you like).

Back to the myths

COMBINING JOBS

Contrary to the myth, you don't have to list each job separately. This is a significant and highly positive revelation, because CVs which list each job separately often end up becoming too long, too repetitive, and ultimately too boring to get noticed.

HR executives have boredom thresholds just like anyone else, and if they read for the fifth job in a row that you *worked on bank reconciliations* and *conducted variance analysis* then they are more likely to nod off than give you the thumbs up.

Combining jobs not only can help you manage CV length, but also can free you from the perceived necessity to repeat the same type of achievements over and over again. Obviously, you need to pick and choose and combine the right jobs, but, if you do this, the end result is often a more interesting and higher-impact CV.

Please note, I mentioned that you need to combine the *right jobs*. This is significant. You can't just combine them indiscriminately. For example, if you have worked in multiple sectors throughout your career, but are now set on a career in finance and have more recently worked in accountancy, then it is worth keeping your recent accounting jobs separate, but combining your older and less relevant jobs. You always have to keep your target in mind, and use the right formula to best highlight your most relevant and attractive skills and traits for the job in question.

OMITTING JOBS

A surprising amount of people have CVs which are far too long. I think the record CV I have seen is thirty pages. The owner of this CV was probably proud of its length, but it was a false pride because the CV was far too long to be effective, and certainly didn't get results. The reason people end up with CVs which are too long is partly because some careers span many jobs, and partly because some rule-mongers bandy about ridiculous CV-writing myths, prodding unwitting job seekers to dutifully add entries onto their CV after each and every new job until they end up with a document which is biblical in proportions, and, as far as its effectiveness as a career document is concerned, is only good enough for the bin.

While this may sound shocking to some people, one of the most proactive things you could do to your CV is actually to get rid of older and less relevant jobs. Personally speaking, I am not adverse to completely removing jobs which do not add any value to the CV, especially older jobs. Saying that, some people are a bit more timid, and still leave the briefest of entries along the lines of: *'1995 to 1996 worked as a cashier for Sainsbury's'*.

Of course, some advisers will tell you in no uncertain terms that the employer will need to know your full job history from leaving school to the current day. However, this too is arguable, and my response (again with my employer's hat on) is that this assertion is rather naive. Many employers are used to (and are actually thankful for) candidates summarising their career history rather than going overboard with it. Besides, it is highly unlikely that you will be denied an interview on the basis that you didn't go back far enough in your career to list old, irrelevant jobs. As mentioned, the vast majority of employers are primarily looking for what you can do for them now, not nitpicking about what you did or didn't do just after you left school. As long as you make it clear to the employer that you have all the skills that he or she is looking for, and you do this in a sufficiently concise and legible manner, then this is far more important than condemning another tree to the sawmill for the sake of appeasing an outdated, largely impractical and frequently counterproductive myth.

Yes, it is true that if you combine or omit jobs then some employers may occasionally wonder about the specifics. However, at least you have their interest, and if they are that bothered about the nitty-gritty then they can always ask you about minor points at interview.

This is far better than the alternative of submitting a long, repetitive and boring CV, which has far less chance of being picked up and read in the first place, let alone arousing the employer and stimulating him or her enough to secure you an interview.

I have included a practical section in Chapter 7 to give you some hands-on experience of this. If you are intending to write your own CV then it will be worth your while trying your hand at this section.

Firm objections – company profiles

Going to work for a large company is like getting on a train – are you going 60 miles an hour, or is the train going 60 miles an hour and you're just sitting still? J. PAUL GETTY

Statute 77 (according to the Southwell CV Society): 'CVs should include company profiles'

Including company profiles or snippets of information about each company you have worked for is actually relatively rare on UK CVs. Saying that, this doesn't prevent certain myth-mongers from insisting, to anyone daft enough to listen, that it is an absolute necessity. Of course, it is nothing of the sort, and rarely adds true value to a CV.

The reason for this is again based in common sense. As you should know by now, you only have so much space to sell your skills on a CV, so if you use up a few precious lines per job entry talking about the history, turnover and demographics of every company you have worked for then effectively you are just eating away at the valuable space you have left to sell your own skills and traits. What's more, do you really think that busy HR executives give a fig that Nestlé has operations on four different continents and in several different time zones? As surprising as this may seem to some people, when employers read your CV they are actually more interested in you and what you can do for them, not how much money some of the companies you have worked for made in the last financial year.

Order disorder – section positioning

One of the advantages of being disorderly is that one is constantly making exciting discoveries. A. A. MILNE

Amendment 15 subsection D (Roehampton Roughneck résumé rituals): 'CVs need to be ordered a certain way'

It is noticeable that many people use the same sections but order their CVs differently. While I myself have a preference for ordering, at least it is part of a flexible approach; I am open-minded about changing the ordering in certain circumstances if this gives the application more weight. For example, sometimes I move the qualifications section higher up the CV if the client is a student or graduate with limited work experience. If you talk to some advisers they will tell you that qualifications sections for new graduates always need to be right near the top of the CV, between the profile and the work experience section. There is sense in this, and it is often a good ploy. However, as mentioned, it often pays to be more open-minded, and in some circumstances it is more advantageous to take a different approach. For instance, some graduates also have a significant amount of relevant work experience. Given the fact that employers often value hands-on work experience more than theoretical academic study, in some cases it is advantageous to prioritise this work experience over and above academic work.

Another section which seems to change place depending upon the author of the CV is the skills section. My own preference for this is to place it towards the end of the CV, and this is probably the most popular place. However, a fair proportion of people prefer to place their skills section near the top of their CV. I have asked people (including some recruiters) why they do this, and most of the time they cannot come up with an answer, let alone any logical explanation. However, a minority of people I have spoken to have at least suggested a couple of reasons. The first one goes along the lines of *'Employers are very busy people and they don't have time to read a full CV, and so it's best to summarise the skills right at the top.'* Another strange comment I received once from a so-called résumé expert in America was that it is best to put skills at the top of a CV because 'employers always read CVs bottom-up!'

I passed on these comments to some HR executives who confirmed the fact that they were busy, but nevertheless also scoffed at the accusation that they only read skills sections (and do so back to front). In fact, many HR executives are not satisfied by skills sections alone, and really need proof of expertise in the skills advertised elsewhere in the body of the CV. Significantly, this is one main reason why placing your skills section at the end of your CV rather than at the beginning is often more effective. If you add skills at the very beginning then at that point they read as unsubstantiated claims. On the other hand, if you do your groundwork and firstly introduce these skills as real examples in the work experience section, then by the time you summarise these skills towards the end of the CV they are no longer unsubstantiated claims but are instead a reiteration of genuine attributes you have already backed up with concrete work examples. As such they are more powerful, and are usually more effective.

There are other sections, too, whose ordering seems interchangeable from CV to CV. These include the name and contact details, interests, date of birth and more. Some people will undoubtedly tell you that certain sections of the CV need to be in a cast-iron particular order. However this, like many of the examples above, is just a myth.

If it's possibly broke, maybe think bespoke

The chains of habit are too weak to be felt until they are too strong to be broken. SAMUEL JOHNSON

Sometimes it pays to include extra sections, if appropriate. For example, I write CVs for entrepreneurs, consultants etc, and on occasion the inclusion of unusual sections has proved fruitful, e.g. *testimonials* and *company profile* (as in for their own company). Similarly, depending on the circumstances, I occasionally include sections such as '*professional memberships*' and '*awards*'. Again, there is no set formula for this, and a lot of it comes from experience and knowing how best to accentuate the positives for a client given his or her particulars, CV space constraints and the job in question.

Questionable advice – recruiters

I am not one of those who in expressing opinions confine themselves to facts. WEARING WHITE CLOTHES (MARK TWAIN)

I hope the above sections about myths will have opened your eyes to the absolute fact that some CV advice is given whimsically without thought or foundation. Obviously, if someone offers you advice it's entirely up to you whether or not you want to take any notice of it. However, at the very least, I would suggest that you ask the adviser in question to explain the rationale behind it. If they can't give you a convincing and logical answer it probably suggests they haven't really thought about it properly.

I think I should point out that while some recruiters do come in for a bit of stick in this book (due to the shoddy and ill-conceived advice that certain recruiters spout), I certainly would not want to tar all recruiters with the same brush and therefore should also mention that many recruiters do give out far better advice. Indeed, I have had numerous enlightening discussions with recruiters myself. However, just as in most industries some companies are better than others, the same applies in recruitment, and some recruiters are better, and more knowledgeable than others. In the above sections I have given you not only more food for thought, but also the rationale behind it based on logic and common sense. If you now receive instructions from one of the lesser recruitment agencies suggesting you change your CV in a particular way then at the very least you should be better placed to judge the true value of this *advice*, and be in a better position to decide for yourself if their recommendations are right for you or not.

6

The most asked CV questions – and some you hadn't thought about

CV questions and answers

Learn all you can from the mistakes of others. You won't have time to make them all yourself.

ALFRED SHEINWOLD

... hopefully yet more extremely useful CV advice that you were possibly previously oblivious to ...

In the course of my work I have received and answered a great many questions pertaining to jobs, careers and CVs. This section lists just a selected sample of actual questions and answers.

Q. Overselling I know that I have all the skills that I say I do, but I don't want to come across as big-headed. Do you think I should include them all or leave some out?

A. *Actually, I think you may be doing yourself a disservice here. Your achievements and skills are significant, and I can tell you without fear of contradiction that a lot of people with less experience than you are actually shouting about their experience a lot louder (and remember you do need to sell yourself). Admittedly, some people do shout louder than they should – and I wouldn't recommend that. However, looking at what you have done, and the results you have achieved, then you are perfectly entitled to not only reveal, but actually showcase these achievements in the shop window. You are someone with a track record of success, and it would be a shame if by omitting genuine achievements out of modesty this went under the employer's radar.*

Q. Technical CV Do technical CVs just need to include technical details?

A. *I have viewed thousands of technical CVs over the years, and many have such a heavy technical slant that the candidate's personality doesn't come through. One thing you need to remember is that not every person who reads your CV will be as au fait with technical aspects as you are, and if you concentrate totally on the technical aspects then you risk alienating yourself if your CV falls into the hands of a non-technical decision maker. Moreover, even if* the employer is very technically-minded, it is still important to give him or her an indication about what you can bring to the table as a person. After all, a lot of very technical jobs still have social elements, requiring you to connect with clients, users, teams, colleagues and stakeholders. You should remember that employers want to see how you fit in as a full package in the workplace as a whole, and not just in your own little pigeon-hole.

Q. Project detail Will it give me an advantage if I can go into greater detail about my domain knowledge and legacy project?

A. *It is all about getting the balance right. Yes, you could delve into the nitty-gritty and go into great detail talking about the finer aspects of a particular project, but you should ask yourself if this is really necessary. Especially as it will take up a lot of valuable space. Employers often get a lot of CVs to look through. At this first point of contact the main thing is to quickly demonstrate your expertise and your relevant achievements, rather than getting bogged down with explaining finer technical details. If you are applying for a technical job then of course you will need to demonstrate technical ability, but as mentioned you need to get the balance right on your CV.*

There is sometimes a fine line between highlighting your technical skills and overloading your CV with superfluous information, so you need to be careful not to overstep the mark.

Q. Adding achievements Is it best to add achievements after the rest of the CV?

A. *No. It is best to include achievements as you are actually writing the CV.*

Effectively, there is a lot more to CV writing than meets the eye, and it is often a fine balancing act if you want to achieve the strongest possible document within a short, restricted space.

You can't include everything if you want to maintain optimum length, so choices need to be made about what to exclude as well as what to include (i.e. it isn't just a simple matter of adding things on willy-nilly).

If you wait until you have finished everything else before writing your all-important achievements, the chances are that you will be left with just a very small amount of space to fit in your trump cards. This doesn't make sense. If compromises have to be made then the first thing to go should be the things with the least weight, not those that add most value.

It is best to have all of the pieces of the jigsaw on the table right from the onset and before you start putting it all together. If, instead, you hold some of the pieces back, then it is a pretty much impossible job.

Q. IT skills I have acquired lots of experience with many IT programs over the years. What is the best way to mention all these?

A. *There is more to CV writing and job applications than meets the eye. The most effective applications are not those which say as much as possible, but those which tell the employer things that he or she wants to hear in a concise, pertinent and proactive manner.*

If you are in IT then programs are important. However, you should still think twice before simply listing all your experience willy-nilly.

You also need to consider that if you just list all your programs, then this will not only increase the length of your CV, but what frequently happens is that it makes the more important programs less obvious to potential employers.

The best thing to do is to be selective about the programs you mention, and tweak your CV depending upon the job in question. So if the employer is primarily interested in .net and SQL then there is little value including a big long list of legacy programs that he or she isn't interested in.

As you will note on the document returned to you, we have already included the most important programs for this job. Not only that but we have incorporated these into the achievements, and as such they are more powerful than if they were just placed in a skills section. Abilities which are shown as examples in achievements always trump mere lists of skills.

Q. Different opinions I've asked four different people about my CV and they all have different opinions. Who should I believe?

A. *Everyone has an opinion about any art form, not just written documents. And CVs, like any written document, are subjective to some degree and thus open to different interpretations.*

I know from my work, research, discussions and feedback that CVs which are written flexibly and creatively with the job in mind tend to be more effective than those which are based on habits and myths which haven't been really thought out or analysed properly.

One good tip would be to ask any adviser about the logic behind his or her advice. Many advisers are suddenly struck dumb by the simple question 'Why?' This in itself should tell you something. Other advisers do try to explain, but usually just quote a myth rather than explain with real logic and rationale. It isn't a very persuasive argument to just conveniently say 'because that's how employers like it'. A persuasive argument would explain not only why they like it, but also why they like it more than the alternative(s). If he or she can back it up with research and results then all the better. However, it's unlikely that you will find any typical adviser who has done any real research on what works best with CVs; from what I have seen, most just quote myths.

Q. CV length I think the main problem with my CV is that it is too long. What do you think?

A. *People often talk about CV page length as if it is the main difference between them landing a good job or not. This is a rather simplistic view. In fact, top-quality CVs are multifaceted, and comprise a great many carefully selected and especially blended ingredients. Page length is just one of a great many factors, although it is not insignificant by any means. Each small piece of the jigsaw is extremely significant and contributes to the success of the CV, and ultimately your job prospects.*

Just as haute cuisine derives from a perfect mix of quality ingredients and the magic touch of top experienced chefs, the same can be said of job-winning CVs, because job-winning CVs can only be crafted with a full set of ingredients, the perfect recipe, and experienced and talented writing.

Page length therefore is just one tiny ingredient of many (albeit a very important one).

Q. CV priorities Are some parts of a CV more important than others?

A. *Yes, some parts of a CV are more important than others. Moreover, there are potential conflicts if you are not careful. You really need to consider and prioritise fundamentals when weighing up your CV and decide what to include, focus on or even omit altogether.*

To elaborate: in the whole scheme of things CV length carries a higher weight than many other aspects. Actually, this is quite natural, and arguably inevitable, because CV length is an immediate visible contributor to overall first impressions, whereas issues such as whether or not you split jobs out separately do not have the same impact on first impressions. Indeed, the perception of numerous so-called issues is often out of sync with the reality. Many so-called CV rules are ignored or completely overlooked by employers when they read a CV, regardless of what some advisers or lesser recruiters will tell you.

This is an important point because if you give more priority to less important parts of your CV then this can (and often does) adversely affect something more fundamental. For example, if you compromise good CV length just to accommodate the myth that you need to include all jobs and spit them all out then your CV's ability as an effective job application tool will almost inevitably suffer.

Q. Adding essentials If it says 'essential' on a job specification is that flexible?

A. *I have asked HR executives about such issues in the past, and the general response has been that if they state that something is 'essential' in the job specification, they usually mean it. Some HR executives have told me that they would immediately discount someone who doesn't fulfil all the essentials in the job specification. Of course, you are quite within your rights to apply for any job, but it is worth remaining realistic about your prospects nevertheless.*

As it happens, it is very rare that I see a job applicant who doesn't tick the vast majority of the job specifications' essential and desirable boxes. Proof in itself (if ever it was needed) that competition for jobs is indeed very strong.

Q. Voluntary work I would also be interested in your opinion on whether it would be beneficial to mention my journey to Mongolia in a 1988, 1 litre Fiat Panda as it raised money for charity and involved brief voluntary work with a Mongolian orphanage?

A. *As far as your charity work is concerned, it really depends on the job you are applying for. If it was for a charity or an NGO sector organisation for example then I would have definitely included it. However, if you are targeting finance, the finance sector is a bit* more hard-nosed. Significantly, finance employers look for dedicated professionals who could do a good job for them. The inclusion of your long trip could even be disadvantageous because it could be perceived that you may be inclined to go off on long trips, and not devote enough time to learning and progressing within the company. Obviously, this is a bit of a generalisation and not every single finance employer will see it this way, but it is significant nonetheless. If you have some work experience which is more relevant for the finance sector, you would be better off concentrating on including that.

Q. Skills I wondered if there was value in putting the skills I acquired at each job under the heading of the relevant job title?

A. *This is a classic case of overdoing things. It is a repetitive and relatively ineffective way of selling yourself. It is also more common for people with unimpressive work histories to do this, rather than those going for good professional jobs. Any claims you make re skills without context remain just claims. As such, they are weak. However, if you instead manage to demonstrate relevant skills by weaving them into your real-life work experience then this is far more powerful. If you do it this way they are no longer just claims, but proven examples of your capabilities. This adds far more value than just a list of skills you have learned. Yes, you could add both, but it will make your CV unnecessarily long and repetitive, and increase the danger of boring the reader.*

Q. Titles Currently the title in my profile is 'Commercial Director', but I've had other roles too so do you think it would carry more weight by combining it to e.g. 'Commercial Director/Strategic Investments Director'?

A. *There are a lot of considerations to think about even for something as simple as a title. For example, space is one factor. In your case is there enough space to add 'strategic investments director'? Saying that, it really depends on the job you are targeting. If you are just targeting a commercial director job and the job specification mentions 'commercial director' but not 'strategic investments director' then I would definitely just keep it as 'commercial director'. However, if the job specification mentions 'strategic investments director' then if you have space it is worth including.*

Another thing you need to consider in cases like this is that often employers are looking for specialists in a particular area, and if you include a generic title to cover more bases then the trade-off is that it weakens your speciality message.

Q. Achievements Is it a good idea to restrict the number of achievements in case the CV looks too 'meaty'?

A. *There is no doubt whatsoever that you will be competing against senior professionals who are selling themselves to the hilt, so if you want to compete effectively you also need to sell yourself and come across as an achiever. Yes, you could tone down the achievements both in terms of quantity and substance. However, if you do this it may be counterproductive.*

You only have so much space to sell yourself on the CV, and really you need to take full advantage of both horizontal and vertical space. Obviously, you need to be careful not to disturb legibility; and bullet points and neat single-line entries will help in this respect. However, as long as it looks presentable then there is nothing wrong with including plenty of achievements. Indeed, the actual number of achievements you include is significant. Not only do they help illustrate and reaffirm your expertise, but they are even useful on a psychological level; effectively the number of achievements is a clear visual indication to the employer that the candidate is an achiever.

Q. Highlighting figures Would you advise displaying any benefits in value or numeric terms together in one area? That way I can give a quick overview of the measureable benefits and achievements.

A. *If you do this it will probably come across as artificial. Obviously, we deal with many CVs day in day out. Now and again we do receive CVs from people who go out of their way to highlight particular things, be it figures, IT programs or whatever. The usual way they do this is by highlighting figures in bold font or by creating a separate section and clumping all the figures together. Either way, it looks unconventional and over-conspicuous.*

It's also unnecessary. If your CV is presentable then employers should be able to read all about your impressive figures quite naturally in the body of your achievements without you trying to force-feed them.

Q. Profile How will I be able to fully back up my personal statement in my IT CV?

A. CVs are not meant to be legal documents that are scrutinised by a court of law. An employer probably won't ask you to provide physical evidence of what you say in a profile. However, you should be upfront and honest about your skills; so if you do not possess the skills mentioned in the profile then you should omit them.

If you do indeed possess significant skills and experience then there is nothing wrong with including these. In the unlikely event that an employer will give you an in-depth interrogation on each and every point on your profile during interview, all you need do is give examples to back up what you say. So for example, if you are applying for an IT job, then when you are preparing for your interview you could formulate some answers just in case you get asked questions relating to your expertise in e.g. servers, systems and networks.

Q. Little experience My CV seems a little short so should I try to make it longer by expanding on my qualifications at the top because I think one page is too short?

A. CVs which are two pages long are a good length for many people. However, there is no point in having a two-page CV just for the sake of it; you need to play to your strengths. In your case it is pointless having a weak two-page CV when you can have a far more powerful one-page CV. If you had more experience and could carry a two-page CV, then that would be all well and good. But you don't. All you are doing is padding out your CV with some weak entries such as all your degree modules. This is not going to impress an employer. They are more interested in you and what you can offer them, rather than the modules you took for your degree (which in your case are not even relevant to the job in question). If you send out this CV, employers may not even read as far as the important entries, because they may not be sufficiently impressed by the new weaker entries you have now placed at the top of the all-important first page.

Q. Adding colour I think black-and-white CVs look boring, I'm thinking of adding more colours and graphics. What do you think?

A. Essentially, CVs, like any written document are subjective to some degree – and beauty is in the eye of the beholder and all that

– and some people do use brightly coloured CVs with graphics etc. However, a key element to consider is it's not necessarily your own personal preferences that count; the most important thing is what <u>employers</u> prefer. And there is little doubt that on the whole employers do tend to prefer CVs that are concise, legible, well structured, professional looking and printed with black ink on white or light-coloured paper. Yes, you could add colour and images and use unusual fonts, and your CV will indeed be perceived as different – but frequently 'different' in the sense of conspicuous and unusual rather than professional and outstanding.

Yes, a more unusual looking CV may help you get noticed – just not always in the sense you hoped. All in all it's quite a risky strategy, and unless you really know what you're doing you are better off playing safe.

Over the years I've seen many attempts of candidates trying to stand out by using unusual formats rather than the quality of what they say and how they say it on their CV. With the odd very rare exception such CVs usually come across as artificial, contrived or messy. Occasionally I have seen well-presented original-looking CVs created by professional designers. And if you are looking for work as a graphic designer then this is one area where it might pay to try the unusual – as long as you can pull it off. This is easier said than done, because you need to get the balance right and the usual trade-off with the better looking bespoke graphic designer CVs I have seen is that they frequently afford less space for the all-important CV content. This is a significant point because you still need to sell yourself. Unsurprisingly, even a lot of highly talented graphic designers therefore still use a more conventional CV format when applying for jobs.

Q. Numbering Do we need to number the pages or repeat the header information on pages 2 and 3?

A. Some people do that, but it is by no means obligatory. Personally speaking, I feel it is unnecessary and only detracts from the really important things. Employers are more concerned with what you can do for them rather than repeating headers or telling them what the page number is. Besides, if your CV is so long that employers get confused with the ordering of pages then this tells you something significant – your CV is too long!

Q. Entrepreneurs Is it a good thing to mention my previous self-employment and entrepreneurial skills?

A. *This is a good point. In many cases it can be a disadvantage to flaunt entrepreneurial acumen on a CV. One prime reason for this is that many employers are wary of self-employed people and entrepreneurs. Some are afraid that if they employ them then they will be more likely to leave the job after a short while. Some employers are also scared of the prospect of training an entrepreneur, just in case he or she sets up a rival business at a later date. These fears are all understandable because this sort of thing does happen sometimes.*

However, as with all aspects of CV writing, you need to have an open mind and be flexible. Some jobs actually require entrepreneurial skills. For example, I have seen job specifications for business development managers where the employer has specifically mentioned entrepreneurial skills as a requirement. In such cases it would actually be an advantage to highlight self-employed status and entrepreneurial acumen. My advice therefore would be to consider the job and weigh up the pros and cons of highlighting entrepreneurial prowess based on the actual job and the job requirements. You are under no obligation to mention every skill you possess on your CV.

Q. Skills and key competencies What is the difference between skills and key competencies sections? (Question from an IT professional.)

A. *The skills entries typically highlight your expertise for the job in question. These tend to be abilities which you have acquired through your professional or academic experience. Key competencies are more natural traits and not only reinforce your suitability for the job, but also give the employer an insight into your personality.*

Many DIY CVs in IT only include technical skills; in fact many we receive don't even have that, they just list programs (with no indication of proficiency), and usually a good proportion of these programs are no longer relevant to the job. When an employer considers your CV he or she not only wants to get an idea of your work experience, but also wants to find out about you and what you can offer. It is therefore advantageous if you can go beyond a simple list of programs and show the employer that you have something extra to bring to the table.

Q. Achievement sequence What order do you recommend for work experience achievements: chronological, relevance to the job, kind of achievement, etc?

A. *The ordering of achievements is more important than many people realise. When I write CVs I always pay attention to the ordering of achievements and so should you.*

While it is more conventional for the work experience section as a whole to be chronologically ordered, as with other areas of CV writing there are no hard and fast rules regarding the ordering of work experience achievements for a particular job. You could put them in reverse chronological order if you so desire. However, you need to bear in mind that the purpose of your application is not to tell the employer exactly in which order you did a particular task, but to try to land an interview for your target job. If you consider that many employers will not read to the end of your CV if you do not make a good first impression, then it makes sense to put your most impressive and relevant achievements at the top. The same applies at the other end of the scale too. For example, some achievements do a better job of rounding off than other entries.

Q. Superseded skills Do I need to include all of my job roles in my CV?

A. *Contrary to what some people think, the purpose of your CV is not to list every last aspect of every last job, but to get you interviews. To do this you need to tell the employer what he or she is looking for, rather than fall into the trap of just listing information which they will probably consider superfluous anyway. Yes, you could be more specific, and mention all those old legacy projects, but if you do it could be counterproductive, especially since those programs have no relevance to the job you are now applying for. Moreover, your recent projects (which are all mentioned on your CV) not only supersede the legacy projects, but are far more impressive and relevant.*

Q. Agencies I want to apply to recruitment agencies. Should I make my CV generic?

A. *Agencies tend to look on generic CVs more favourably than real employers, but I would personally advise anyone wanting to provide a generic CV to consider the implications before rushing into things. At the very least, consider narrowing down the options as much as* *possible. The reason for this is that while it is a good thing to be versatile, there is a threshold and once you pass that, you risk becoming a 'jack of all trades' rather than a specialist in a particular field.*

We sometimes get inquiries from people who want a generic CV covering e.g. all of the following: banking, accounting, investments and stockbroking. This is all well and good, but if an employer is looking for a top accountant then they are more likely to sit up and take notice of a specialist accountant CV than a generic CV.

With this in mind, there is actually a bit of a catch-22 situation if you rely on recruitment agencies for your job search. The obvious temptation for such an approach is to make your CV generic, because if you do so you are more likely to generate more matches with the recruitment agency software. However, once your CV goes in front of a real employer then unless versatility is high on the employer's agenda, you would probably be better off presenting a more specifically targeted CV.

Of course, it is entirely up to you how you go about your job search, and you will need a top quality CV regardless of whether you choose to go through recruitment agencies or make direct applications yourself. Nevertheless, I would try to take as much control over my career decisions as possible. This means being selective about which jobs to apply for, and applying in a more effective and constructive way for the jobs which do meet your criteria. Note that I mention your criteria (i.e. what is important for you), not just what a recruitment agency wants to offer you. Sometimes there is a discrepancy between the two, and people often do not realise how much until it is too late.

Q. Failure I have sent my CV out for loads of jobs via numerous agencies without success. What do you think the problem is?

A. *Before even looking at your CV, one thing which has struck me is that you seem to be playing a numbers game and applying for far too many jobs which are, in all probability, significantly different if you analyse them all. This is not the best way to land jobs for a variety of reasons. First, different employers look for different things, so if you send off the same CV for different jobs then by definition you will almost certainly be ignoring some of the things that employers are looking for. Although many people think that the more jobs they* *apply for the better, this can often be counterproductive. Often your chances of landing jobs will increase if you narrow down your search, be more selective with the jobs you apply for, and amend your CV slightly each time towards the job specification in question. That way you are actually addressing what the employer is looking for. If you do not consider the employer properly, your chances of landing the job diminish greatly.*

Q. Assessing CVs I have heard so many different opinions on what a good CV should include and look like – who do I believe?

A. *I agree with you in that many people offer a wide variety of differing opinions. This is part of the problem. Too many people are adamant that their particular format is 100 per cent right, when in reality there are a lot less rights and wrongs than people make out.*

If there is one constant it is that opinions differ, and that it is inevitable that not everyone will agree. This is especially so since some aspects of the CV such as presentation are subjective. However, there are nevertheless certain areas that most people agree upon. For example, that the CV should be a good length (two pages maximum), it should be legible, use bullet points, be relevant to the job, sell your skills, etc.

Even then you will still get some people (usually lesser recruiters) who disagree on even the most basic fundamental points. One tip I would give you therefore is not to believe everything someone says just because they work in recruitment or did a stint as a career coach.

If what someone tells you is contradictory or doesn't seem to make sense then if you ask for an explanation they should be able to explain their rationale clearly and logically. If they can't then the quality of the advice could be put into question.

Q. Ambiguous job My current CV isn't working. How do I target it for 'managerial business/technical' in the IT sector?

A. *As you can appreciate the above job types are not the same and would require your CV to be optimised differently. If you have something specific in mind it would be best if you could be more specific with your requirements.*

When you state 'managerial business/technical' what do you mean? Is it general management, project management, business development management, business analysis or something else? Your current

CV isn't focused and is sending out mixed messages. It sounds like you are not really sure what your own specialisation is. Yes, I can optimise it for a particular job, but first you really need to decide for yourself which direction you wish to take.

Q. Complex job history I have had many previous jobs. Is this a disadvantage if I list them all on my CV?

A. *If you have had many previous jobs then all this work experience can be to your advantage. However, on the negative side, an employer may interpret this as an indication that you are someone who will not stick around for long.*

You have to judge each situation separately and weigh up the pros and cons depending on your work history and the job in question. If you think that a long list of previous jobs will be a disadvantage then you may need to rework your CV. If you can still put across the many benefits you offer without giving the impression that you are a job hopper then this could work to your advantage. One option you have to rework this section is to actually omit some of your less relevant jobs. There is no cast-iron rule which says you have to include every last job on your CV.

Another thing which you can do is to club jobs together. For example, if you have had two stints at one company, rather than list them separately you can blend the dates and club them together as one entry.

Q. Over the top I know that I need to sell myself in the profile but I am wary of adding too many impressive adjectives in case it sounds over the top. Should I tone it down?

A. *In my experience the vast majority of people undersell themselves in profiles. While you need to be comfortable with what you write, and should only highlight your genuine traits and skills, if you have a lot to offer an employer and can back this up elsewhere in your CV, then there is no reason why you should not shout about it.*

Q. Repetition If I mention skills in my skills section which have previously been mentioned elsewhere in my CV will this not be too repetitive?

A. *Sometimes people repeat job entries over and over again lots of times throughout the CV, especially if they have done the same type of job at different companies. This isn't really very productive, as it will just send the reader to sleep. However, briefly highlighting skills isn't really the same as repeating work entries, and personally I wouldn't be too concerned. First, skills sections are conventional, very common, widely recognised and generally accepted. This is totally understandable; after all, you are just briefly highlighting and subtly reinforcing skills of interest to the employer. It's not as if you are saying the same sentences over and over again.*

Q. Quantifying skills Should I quantify skills in the skills section?

A. *This is not normally done. It is generally recommended to quantify and qualify achievements in the work experience section, but entries in the skills section are generally left as skills, in their original form, with no additional quantifying. While there is no rule saying you cannot quantify skills in the skills section if you want to – it is entirely your prerogative – my view is that this is not necessary, and that the best place to quantify achievements is the work experience section.*

Q. Personal choice What length would you choose for your own CV?

A. *If I ever needed a CV I'd make it one page and no longer. No doubt about it.*

Q. Aiming wide I have a lot experience in many fields: as the old saying goes, jack of all trades, master of none. How do I prepare my CV so that I can position my talents/experience in such a way that I do not limit my job opportunities with one résumé.

A. *Your problem is that in wanting to keep your options open your CV becomes more generic, and the more generic it is the more diluted and less powerful it is when applying for particular jobs. You need to remember that whenever you apply for a job in a particular field you will be competing against specialists in that field, so while a generic CV may be useful, it is rarely the best option.*

In an ideal world you should submit a top quality targeted and fully optimised CV each and every time. I realise that this is not always possible as not everyone has the time, resources or ability to tailor a different CV for every job application. If you really insist upon keeping all your options open and having a generic CV, I would recommend that at the very least you do two things:

- Design a top quality, relatively generic (but not overly generic) CV, optimised with the transferable skills most appropriate to the jobs you seek. Please note, I recommend that you limit this to a maximum of three job types, or better still just two. You can amend this as appropriate for each job application.
- Craft a top quality targeted CV, professionally optimised for your preferred job or career.

I do not recommend that you maintain a lack of focus and direction in your job search. On the contrary, I suggest that you take the time to examine your needs, aspirations and options, and focus on the one job which you are really suited for, not the many which are not quite right for you.

Q. How to write the best CV What would you say is the most important aspect of a CV?

A. There are many elements which have to all come together in harmony to create a top quality CV. Most people think they can write a good CV just as long as they can make it look presentable and ensure the spelling and grammar are okay. However, there is far more to it. First, even if the presentation is good, the content is more important. There is no point spending hours refining the look of your CV if what you have to say is not well worded, does not sell your skills, or says the wrong kind of things.

If you really want to write a top quality CV then all of the following factors are essential: presentation, direction, format, balance, message and content. You should note that all these factors can themselves be subdivided. For example spelling, grammar, wording, substance, impact, and relevance are just several facets of good content.

The next chapter on writing skills should help you with many of the factors mentioned in the answer to the last question.

7

Develop your CV
writing skills

... how to write far more powerfully than you did previously ...

✓ Writing what is relevant

Existence is no more than the precarious attainment of relevance in an intensely mobile flux of past, present, and future. SUSAN SONTAG

If you have ever picked up a long, wordy document, took one look at it, let out a tired sigh then hurriedly put it straight back down again in favour of a more palatable read then you are not alone. Indeed, thousands of employers do just this on a daily basis with CVs.

When it comes to reading CVs the vast majority of people prefer something concise, legible and presentable. This raises the question of why so many people send off job applications with big, beefy, monsters of CVs. This is certainly a conundrum, but it doesn't stop job hunters from doing it nonetheless.

Many people are well aware of the fact that their CV is too long, too complicated, too messy and too unstructured. However, knowing it and being able to do something positive about it is not quite the same thing. I have lost count of the people who have come to me for help fully conscious of the fact that they have a problem, but without the necessary skill and experience to do anything positive about it.

Hands-on session

So, let us start at the beginning of CV writing with a simple exercise. Before you start writing reams about each job you have ever had, you should ask, *'Are they all relevant?'* Imagine you are applying for work as a salesperson and your work record was as listed below. What could you do to allay the impression that you are a job hopper? Have a think about this and write down your ideas on a piece of paper as you read through the example.

Jan 2007–present	Salesman, ABC Limited
Sep 2006–Jan 2007	Unemployed
Jul 2006–Sep 2006	Painter & Decorator, Painter & Co
Feb 2006–Jun 2006	Salesman, ABC Limited
Apr 2004–Jan 2006	Salesman, HJK Group
Jan 2004–Apr 2004	Driver, Fastcabs
Apr 2003–Jan 2004	Salesman, Salescorp
Feb 2002–Mar 2003	Barman, Raby Arms
Jun 2001–Jan 2002	Telesales Executive, Wire Solutions
Apr 2001–Jun 2001	Unemployed
Feb 2000–Apr 2001	Barman, Raby Arms

This original list has a lot of jobs; too many really. You are not obliged to mention each and every job. Thus I removed less relevant work entries:

Step one

Jan 2007–present	Salesman, ABC Limited
~~Sep 2006–Jan 2007~~	~~Unemployed~~
~~Jul 2006–Sep 2006~~	~~Painter & Decorator, Painter & Co~~
Feb 2006–Jun 2006	Salesman, ABC Limited
Apr 2004–Jan 2006	Salesman, HJK Group
~~Jan 2004–Apr 2004~~	~~Driver, Fastcabs~~
Apr 2003–Jan 2004	Salesman, Salescorp
Feb 2002–Mar 2003	Barman, Raby Arms

Jun 2001–Jan 2002	Telesales Executive, Wire Solutions
~~Apr 2001–Jun 2001~~	~~Unemployed~~
Feb 2000–Apr 2001	Barman, Raby Arms

Did you go as far as I did? Or did you go further still? Even after removing obvious irrelevant jobs, there are still arguably too many. I therefore removed two more:

Step two

Jan 2007–present	Salesman, ABC Limited
Feb 2006–Jun 2006	Salesman, ABC Limited
Apr 2004–Jan 2006	Salesman, HJK Group
Apr 2003–Jan 2004	Salesman, Salescorp
~~Feb 2002–Mar 2003~~	~~Barman, Raby Arms~~
Jun 2001–Jan 2002	Telesales Executive, Wire Solutions
~~Feb 2000–Apr 2001~~	~~Barman, Raby Arms~~

One of the main problems with the result is that there are now gaps in the dates. For example, there is now a date gap between Feb 2002 and Mar 2003. Can you think of a possible solution to this problem?

Remember that many so-called CV rules are just myths, so think laterally and don't be afraid to ignore what you may have read in other books.

In a few minutes a computer can make a mistake so great that it would have taken many men many months to equal it. MERLE MEACHAM

I'm guessing this may have stumped some of you, but well done to those who gave it a shot and have come up with a possible solution. One way around this is to omit the months, as follows:

Step three

2007–present	Salesman, ABC Limited
2006	Salesman, ABC Limited
2004 –2006	Salesman, HJK Group
2003–2004	Salesman, Salescorp
2001–2002	Telesales Executive, Wire Solutions

Can you see how this works? Can you see the improvement? Well done to those of you who identified this workaround. Did any of you go even further? Yes? No? Maybe?

If you haven't then think about this some more before continuing.

If two men agree on everything, you may be sure that one of them is doing the thinking. LYNDON B. JOHNSON

Well, one possibility for improving things yet further is to combine the first two jobs, which represent two separate stints at the same company:

Step four

2006–present	Salesman, ABC Limited
2004 –2006	Salesman, HJK Group
2003–2004	Salesman, Salescorp
2001–2002	Telesales Executive, Wire Solutions

As you can see, the new work experience section is not only more compact, but it is more powerful and relevant too. Also, the space saved by excluding less relevant entries can be put to much better use elsewhere. All of this has been done without lying or inventing new dates or job entries, but simply by following the premise that you do not have to include every single last job in your CV. I realise that some people out there may argue that if you do this you are not giving the full picture. And I can understand this. However, I repeat, the purpose of the CV is not to bore the reader with every intimate career detail, but essentially to attract the employer's attention and hopefully land an interview. This is best achieved by being a bit more creative and more focused.

What about your CV?

Could it benefit from some lateral thinking on the job front too? If so – what are you waiting for?

Writing concisely

Conciseness is the sister of talent. ANTON CHEKHOV

Writing concisely isn't a particularly easy discipline to master, especially if you restrict yourself to limited word counts as the top professionals do. However, with thought, method, creativity and practice most people can improve on their ability to write concisely. And even if this isn't enough to refine your six-page CV to two pages without losing its message, power or effectiveness, at least it should help you get it down to perhaps three or four pages. And if you can do this then it is a clear improvement.

The first thing you can do is actually pretty obvious; get rid of anything which is irrelevant or superfluous. Now I can already hear you saying that this doesn't apply to your CV because *it is all relevant*. Of course it is – and you're not the first, and you won't be the last, to say so.

Even so, I have a useful exercise to try, so if you can please just humour me for a while then we may both learn something.

Hands-on session

Regardless of how long your CV is, I would like you to look at it again and identify at least one thing which is superfluous before we move on. There's always an opportunity to make what you say more concise and clear.

I'll just wait here patiently while you look ...

Hopefully, you will have joined in and have examined your CV. If so, thank you for that.

If you have managed to spot one thing that adds no real value, then congratulations, you have taken the first step to writing more concisely.

The second step is pretty obvious once you have mastered the first step, and it is a matter of going through the rest of your CV striking off anything which is not relevant, which is overly repetitive or which doesn't add any value to your CV. Hopefully you should end up with something looking a bit more compact. Given the fact that you are not striking off anything which adds value to your CV then this isn't going to adversely affect the strength of your message. In fact, what you are doing is making your CV more enticing to read without diminishing its power or impact.

If you are a bit unsure of how to go about things, or are still somewhat sceptical about the effectiveness of this technique we can go through an example together below. The example is taken from a real CV, although to conceal the candidate's identity I have changed the details.

Curriculum Vitae

Personal data:
Name: Mark Chambers
Address: 1 Church Row, Norwich, Norfolk
Land line: +44 1632 960678
Date of birth: May 28th. 1969

Matrimonial status:
Married to: Julie Chambers
Children: 1 boy, born May 3rd. 2003

Education:
2000   MBA, Norwich University
Specialty: Supply Chain Strategy. Ranking No. 3 out of 17 students. *[See attachment: MBA.doc]*

Position of trust: President, MBA Alumni Association.
1998   Norwich University, Purchasing Management

PROFESSIONAL CAREER
2006–.
Supply Chain Director ABC Process Engineering Division, VP Supply Chain ABC Process Engineering A/S.
ABC Process Engineering A/S is the Head Quarters of the Process Engineering Division in the Spanish ABC group. It includes 63 companies and +5000 employees and an annual turnover of EUR 1.2 billion.
ABC is the world-market leader in the development, design and engineering of liquid and powder fuels.
Responsibility:
• Direct Spend 885 mill. EUR, Indirect Spend 100 mill. EUR and (but not within direct responsibility) Recovery hours for Engineers 141 mill. EUR.
• 48 managers with approx. 175 staff in the procurement organisation.

The position is originally established based on estimates that there would be considerable financial potential in changing the Procurement Organisation from transactional buying (issuing PO's) to working with sales and development as a strategic partner.

Primary Tasks:
• Drive continuous change process and attitude forward.
• Drive change from local to Global; Creating Global commodity teams within the procurement organisation and driving the organisation towards Low Cost Countries (where applicable).
• Responsible for training and developing the organisation.
• Prepare business cases and decision-making proposals for approval by the Division Board.
• Participate in the most important negotiations.

Two main methods are applied:
- 'Top down' approach for setting strategies, collecting data, KPI's etc.
- Workshops as 'Bottom up' to drive *incentives* in the organisation.

The workshops include Sales, Engineers, Project Managers, Procurement and After Sales from different business areas. (see attachment 'Broadsheet' page 3 'Cover story')

2005–2007
XYZ UK Ltd., Sourcing Manager for computers in Europe & US (based in Manchester).
XYZ manages the daily movements of over 230 million pallets and containers from a global network of over 340 service centres in 65 countries. XYZ's turnover is in the area of 2 billion US$, profit is double that of the NOP group.

Responsibilities:
FMCG:
Global sourcing and development of supply chain solutions for the FMCG segment, interacting and supporting the XYZ sales teams and business leaders in Italy, France, Germany, Belgium, Spain, Mexico and the UK.

Engineering divisions.
Designing and combining innovative supply chain solutions. [See attachment, (page 7) : *Supply Chain.pdf*]

Close collaboration with XYZ Central Planning in New York and Sales teams in order to establish processes, coordinate forecasts, PO's and inventory management. Development of *contingency plans* for all critical product areas.

In general: Most product portfolios are managed with differentiated strategies using supplier segmentation methods and clear processes. There is a strong emphasis in the business on coordination between Sales, Marketing, Finance, Asset Management, Plant Operations, Product Engineering and Sourcing ensuring effective Supplier-to-Customer alignment – ensuring supplies and innovation are main priorities.

Net profit contribution:
+12 M. US$ in 15 months representing 93% of all savings in XYZ Europe Sourcing, covering less than half the total spend.
Company feedback: **[See attachment : *PDP_2006.pdf*]**
Recent PDP (Personal Development Process, originally developed by XYZ) from June 2005:

OVERALL SUBJECTIVE RATING: '*1*', which is the highest possible performance rating given only to the top 5% of the company employees who have 'demonstrated exceptional results...' & 'Demonstrated exceptional behaviour at all times'.

Quotes from PDP process (Overall Performance Dimension):

- 'Mark has demonstrated outstanding combination in both hard and soft skills.

▶

[Details of 4 more jobs omitted]

IT
MS Office package.
Powerpoint.

Language
Spanish: fluent
English: mother tongue
German: basic

Personal qualifications
As a person I am very entrepreneurial, analytical, result- & business orientated, I am
also a facilitator and good at creating personal relations. I am used to multitasking
on a daily basis and to managing and taking decisions under pressure. I appreciate
and cope with challenges, deadlines and cultural dissimilarity. I am driven by
practical results.

Spare time
Good friends, tennis, books, horse riding, DIY & restaurants

Well that was a bit of a mouthful wasn't it? And that was the severely
abridged version. The original was actually considerably longer, but I
cut it down significantly and also conveniently (*ahem*) lost the attach-
ments so as to (hopefully) keep you conscious long enough to wade
through to the end of it – well I did warn you not to get into the
nitty-gritty!

Believe it or not people do actually send off applications using CVs
which are even longer and more cluttered, complicated and unstructured than this one.

As you can see from this candidate's experience and job level, this
person is highly qualified, multilingual with lots of professional experience. He is most obviously both intelligent and talented in his field.
That said, his talents arguably lay in areas other than CV writing.

*So what can we do to improve the length and reduce the clutter of
this CV?*

Below I will list some suggestions of my own, but before you look at them it would be a good exercise if you could read the above CV yet again, and identify for yourself the areas which are superfluous and which could be omitted without devaluing the CV.

Never value the valueless. The trick is to know how to recognise it. SIDNEY MADWED

I hope you will have had a go at this yourself. Now compare your suggestions with mine that follow.

Curriculum Vitae

Personal data:
Name: Mark Chambers
Address: 1 Church Row, Norwich, Norfolk
Land line: +44 1632 960678
Date of birth: May 28th. 1969

~~**Matrimonial status:**~~
~~Married to: Julie Chambers~~
~~Children: 1 boy, born May 3rd. 2003~~

This is taking up several lines to say something which is of no relevance whatsoever to the employer. We can therefore remove it.

Education:
2000   MBA, Norwich University
Specialty: Supply Chain Strategy. ~~Ranking No. 3 out of 17 students. [See attachment: MBA.doc]~~

Another significant point of note is that this candidate is submitting a CV which is already six pages in length, yet on top of that he is also including extra documents. Such weighty applications usually only serve to deter not entice employers to read them.

PROFESSIONAL CAREER
2006–.
Supply Chain Director ABC Process Engineering Division, VP Supply Chain ABC Process Engineering A/S.

There is no real value in purposely including a date on a separate line to the job title. All it does is take up extra space unnecessarily.

All the above doesn't say anything positive or useful about the candidate and isn't adding any value whatsoever to the application. Consequently we can omit it.

Responsibility:
• Direct Spend 885 mill. EUR, Indirect Spend 100 mill. EUR and (but not within direct responsibility) Recovery hours for Engineers 141 mill. EUR.
• 48 managers with approx. 175 staff in the procurement organisation.

The position is originally established based on estimates that there would be considerable financial potential in changing the Procurement Organisation from transactional buying (issuing PO's) to working with sales and development as a strategic partner.

The last four lines above form an unconventional extra paragraph. It looks out of place, and is really just adding to the clutter. Normally such paragraphs can either be taken out, or rewritten as a neater, single-line entry in the achievements section. It really depends on how useful or irrelevant the entry is.

Primary Tasks:
- Drive continuous change process and attitude forward.
- Drive change from local to Global; Creating Global commodity teams within the procurement organisation and driving the organisation towards Low Cost Countries (where applicable).
- Responsible for training and developing the organisation.
- Prepare business cases and decision-making proposals for approval by the Division Board.
- Participate in the most important negotiations.

The above tasks are quite simply just that. They are pretty basic in the whole scheme of things and are not really impressive achievements as they stand. These are some of the things which would need work on for the final version.

Two main methods are applied:
- ~~'Top down'~~ approach for setting strategies, collecting data, KPI's etc.
- Workshops as ~~'Bottom up'~~ to drive *incentives* in the organisation.

The workshops include Sales, Engineers, Project Managers, Procurement and After Sales from different business areas. ~~(see attachment 'Broadsheet' page 3 'Cover story')~~

Again, this section is somewhat unusual and is talking more about methods rather than actual achievements. Additionally, the candidate talks of targets, but in rather vague terms. There is no real way of knowing his personal involvement, and it's also not clear exactly just what was achieved and how. Strangely enough, for such a long section pertaining to his most recent job the candidate has managed to use a great many words, without really highlighting one single personal achievement. This is a clear case of overcomplicating things.

2005–2007
XYZ UK Ltd., Sourcing Manager for computers in Europe & US (based in Manchester).
~~XYZ manages the daily movements of over 230 million pallets and containers from a global network of over 340 service centres in 65 countries.~~
~~XYZ's turnover is in the area of 2 billion US$, profit is double that of the NOP group.~~

Again the above paragraph takes up a lot of vital space but in spite of this it still does not add a single bit of useful information about the candidate personally.

Responsibilities:
FMCG:
Global sourcing and development of supply chain solutions for the FMCG segment, interacting and supporting the XYZ sales teams and business leaders in Italy, France, Germany, Belgium, Spain, Mexico and the UK.

Engineering divisions:
Designing and combining innovative supply chain solutions. ~~[See attachment, (page 7) : *Supply Chain.pdf*]~~

Yet more documents!

Close collaboration with XYZ Central Planning in New York and Sales teams in order to establish processes, coordinate forecasts, PO's and inventory management. Development of *contingency plans* for all critical product areas.

In general: Most product portfolios are managed with differentiated strategies using supplier segmentation methods and clear processes. There is a strong emphasis in the business on coordination between Sales, Marketing, Finance, Asset Management, Plant Operations, Product Engineering and Sourcing ensuring effective Supplier-to-Customer alignment – ensuring supplies and innovation are main priorities.

Net profit contribution:
+12 M. US$ in 15 months representing 93% of all savings in XYZ Europe Sourcing, covering less than half the total spend.
~~Company feedback:~~ **[See attachment : *PDP_2006.pdf*]**
~~Recent PDP (Personal Development Process, originally developed by XYZ) from June 2005:~~

~~OVERALL SUBJECTIVE RATING: '*1*', which is the highest possible performance rating given only to the top 5% of the company employees who have 'demonstrated exceptional results...' & 'Demonstrated exceptional behaviour at all times'.~~

~~Quotes from PDP process (Overall Performance Dimension):~~

~~• 'Mark has demonstrated outstanding combination in both hard and soft skills.~~

The candidate here has added comments from his personal development plan. This is something I've seen before, although on the whole it isn't too common. I find it conspicuous and unnecessary. It's also not particularly effective. It is a bit like a school report, and the comments aren't really backed up or justified. The candidate would be better substantiating any claims of proficiency in the body of the work experience section with real examples and concrete job achievements.

IT
MS Office package.
Powerpoint.

Language
Spanish: fluent
English: mother tongue
German: basic

Personal qualifications
As a person I am very entrepreneurial, analytical, result- & business orientated, I am also a facilitator and good at creating personal relations. I am used to multitasking on a daily basis and to managing and taking decisions under pressure. I appreciate and cope with challenges, deadlines and cultural dissimilarity. I am driven by practical results.

Spare time
Good friends, tennis, books, horse riding, DIY & restaurants

How did you do? Did you make similar amendments? Did you miss any? Did you go even further? As a minimum can you *imagine* what your version would have looked like?

To be in a better position to judge just how well we have done, I'll tidy up my version below, and you can do the same with your (real or imaginary) version.

What does your new edition look like? Presumably better, but how does it compare with my new version of this CV, shown without the crossed-out content?

Curriculum Vitae

Personal data:

Name:	Mark Chambers
Address:	1 Church Row, Norwich, Norfolk
Land line:	+44 1632 960678
Date of birth:	28 May 1969

Education:

2000   MBA, Norwich University. Specialty: Supply Chain Strategy.

PROFESSIONAL CAREER

2006–date **Supply Chain Director ABC Process Engineering Division, VP Supply Chain ABC Process**

Responsibility:
* Direct spend €885m, indirect spend €100m, and (but not within direct responsibility) recovery hours for engineers €141m
* 48 managers with approx. 175 staff in the procurement organisation

The position was originally established based on estimates that there would be considerable financial potential in changing the Procurement Organisation from transactional buying (issuing POs) to working with sales and development as a strategic partner.

Primary Tasks:
* Drive continuous change process and attitude forward.
* Drive change from local to global, creating global commodity teams within the procurement organisation and driving the organisation towards low cost countries (where applicable).
* Responsible for training and developing the organisation.
* Prepare business cases and decision-making proposals for approval by the Division Board.
* Participate in the most important negotiations.

Two main methods are applied:
* 'Top down' approach for developing strategies, collecting data and setting cross company commodity teams, work flows, supplier segmentation understanding, low cost country sourcing, KPIs, etc.
* Workshops as 'Bottom up' to drive incentives in the organisation.

The workshops include Sales, Engineers, Project Managers, Procurement and After Sales.

2005–2007   **XYZ UK Ltd., Sourcing Manager for computers in Europe & US**
Responsibilities:
FMCG:
* Global sourcing and development of supply chain solutions for the FMCG segment, interacting and supporting the XYZ sales teams and business leaders in Italy, France, Germany, Belgium, Spain, Mexico and the UK.

Engineering divisions:
* Designing and combining innovative supply chain solutions.
* Close collaboration with XYZ Central Planning in New York and Sales teams in order to establish processes, coordinate forecasts, POs and inventory management.
* Development of *contingency plans* for all critical product areas.

In general: Most product portfolios are managed with differentiated strategies using supplier segmentation methods and clear processes. There is a strong emphasis in the business on coordination between Sales, Marketing, Finance, Asset Management, Plant Operations, Product Engineering and Sourcing, ensuring effective Supplier-to-Customer alignment – ensuring supplies and innovation are main priorities.

Net profit contribution:
+12m US$ in 15 months representing 93% of all savings in XYZ Europe Sourcing, covering less than half the total spend.

IT Skills
MS Office package.
PowerPoint.

Language
English: native speaker
Spanish: fluent
German: basic

Personal qualifications
As a person I am very entrepreneurial, analytical, result- and business-orientated. I am also a facilitator and good at creating personal relations. I am used to multitasking on a daily basis as well as managing and taking decisions under pressure. Furthermore, I appreciate and cope with challenges, deadlines and cultural dissimilarity. I am driven by practical results.

Spare time
Good friends, tennis, books, horse riding, DIY and restaurants

Effectively, in the latest version we have now gone from what was a (already significantly abridged) 1,000-word document down to a 700-word CV by sheer dint of removing superfluous entries. This is a sizeable difference in word count. Yet not a single jot of value has been lost, because we haven't removed anything which actually contributed to the CV in the first place.

As you can see, while the CV is still far too long, too cluttered and unsuitable for job applications, at the very least it is starting to look a bit more compact, slightly less haphazard, and a tiny bit more enticing to read (and I do mean just a tiny bit).

Writing even more concisely

A sentence should contain no unnecessary words, a paragraph no unnecessary sentences, for the same reason that a drawing should have no unnecessary lines and a machine no unnecessary parts.

WILLIAM STRUNK, JR.

Now that we have discovered the first secret of writing concisely, the next step is to look at what is left and ask ourselves whether it is (a) relevant, (b) not already covered, or (c) needs more added to it.

Sometimes if you do this you will come across paragraphs which are a *bit* relevant, and *maybe just about worth including*. In which case you have to use your initiative and decide whether or not to include them. Additionally, if you do decide to include such paragraphs then they aren't going to be much use in the whole scheme of things left unattended, so you will also need to make them far more pertinent and proactive. It isn't just a matter of leaving them in and making them shorter.

Hands-on session

To demonstrate this let us take a paragraph at random from the above CV.

In general: Most product portfolios are managed with differentiated strategies using supplier segmentation methods and clear processes. There is a strong emphasis in the business on coordination between Sales, Marketing, Finance, Asset Management, Plant Operations, Product Engineering and Sourcing, ensuring effective Supplier-to-Customer alignment – ensuring supplies and innovation are main priorities.

This paragraph is somewhat strange, in that it reads like something taken from a textbook rather than a CV. It is distant and there is no real implication that the candidate himself is involved in any of these activities. That said, the activities mentioned are relevant to the job sector (supply chain management), and in all likelihood he was indeed involved in such activities.

In cases like this the best thing to do would be to consult the candidate to find out whether or not this was something he was actually involved in. If he was not involved then that is something we can discount and remove from the CV. On the other hand, if he was involved then we not only need to make it more concise, but we also need to personalise it, and make it more proactive.

There is actually quite a lot in the paragraph, so it's probably best to summarise it in just two bullet points rather than squash everything onto one line.

How about you trying to do that now? I've had my fill of coffee for today, thank you very much, but it's a good excuse to go and tinkle on my piano while you (hopefully) get stuck in.

Life is like a piano ... what you get out of it depends on how you play it. TOM LEHRER

That was great. I hope you enjoyed trying out this exercise just as much as I enjoyed playing my piano. Ah well, playtime over. Let's get back to work.

For example, we could say this:

- Introduced radical supplier segmentation methods and processes to successfully manage product portfolios
- Successfully prioritised and coordinated sales, marketing, finance, assets, operations and products to improve supplier-to-customer alignment

As you can see, the paragraph is now not only broken up into a better structure, but it is also more proactive. In addition to this, rather than simply listing the activities in a distant, almost detached manner, we have now personalised them so the achievements are attributed to the candidate.

How do your sentences compare? Are they longer? Shorter? Proactive? As relevant? Did you personalise it too? Or is it still somewhat detached?

As another example, let us consider the following paragraph (which was included in the original CV but which fell afoul of the culling process to bring it down to a manageable length for this book – well, I did warn you it was the severely abridged version!):

Responsible for sourcing and establishing a pier-head in P. R. China (and Hong Kong) for purchase of electrical equipment and tools (and items) used in electronics and plastic production. The resource is still used by BVHG. Turnover is currently +3 billion euros. More than 115 factories have been visited during this period.

It is quite conventional for people and even some professional CV companies to include paragraphs like this. Nevertheless, just because people do it, it doesn't mean it is the best way of getting your message across. It isn't. Please try the same exercise with the above paragraph. You can try refining it down to two, or even just one sentence.

You must be getting the swing of this by now. So hopefully your version will be a great improvement on the original.

The conventional view serves to protect us from the painful job of thinking. JOHN KENNETH GALBRAITH

Again with some thought and creativity we can refine this down to something like:

- Successfully established a Chinese pier-head servicing 115 factories, improving purchasing/production and boosting turnover to over €3b

As you can see, we have not only reduced the word count quite dramatically from 53 to 18, but at the same time we have also introduced elements to beef up the achievement into the bargain. For example, the original paragraph mentioned turnover quite passively, whereas the shorter sentence has the increased turnover as a product of the candidate's action. The net effect is to help portray the candidate as an achiever who not only can carry out a task, but also can do it so well that he brings significant benefits to the company.

What we are effectively doing here is selling the candidate and saying more with fewer words. In other words, the aim is to make whole paragraphs more appealing in fewer lines, without compromising the message. Obviously, this takes a lot more time, skill and effort. However, the end result is a CV which looks a lot neater, more legible and more enticing to read. CVs consisting of neatly bulleted single-line achievements are more appealing on the eye, and contribute towards higher impact first impressions. Again this is highly significant and contributes to improved results.

HEY YOU!

Hey, just because we've been working on this example, it doesn't mean I have forgotten about you and your CV. Come on, you're not going to get out of it that easily! So before you read any further, I'd like you to put the book down (carefully avoiding any pools of tea), and have a go at refining some (or better still *all*) paragraph-long achievements in your own CV – just like we've being doing in the above examples.

Okay, okay ... there's time for you to grab a slice of cake first – I'm an author not a despot (at least not according to the sworn confessions of my bedraggled incarcerated subjects) – but after that you really must get on with it.

Promise?

Writing proactively

I knew a man who gave up smoking, drinking and rich food. He was healthy right up to the day he killed himself. JOHNNY CARSON

... most people do not write anywhere near as proactively as they need to on their CV. In fact many people's CVs are largely passive. This section will help give your CV more life, power and impact ...

If you have ever wandered around looking at menus in restaurant windows to decide what to eat, then you will probably be aware of the fact that some dishes and indeed entire menus sound far more appetising than others. This is sometimes even true of dishes which are fundamentally much the same. For example, the idea of *'quiche and salad'* may whet your appetite, but perhaps not quite enough to entice you through the restaurant doors. On the other hand, if a couple of weeks later you walk past the same restaurant and this time read *'home-baked goat's cheese and caramelised onion quiche with organic rocket and cherry tomato salad drizzled with authentic French vinaigrette'* then, while the dish may be exactly the same, the more appealing description may well be enough to tempt you through the threshold this time.

In fact, this isn't surprising, because it is no secret that marketeers deliberately go out of their way to embellish a product description if they want to boost sales. For example, some of you will be familiar with the Marks & Spencer *'This is not just food, this is M&S food'* advertising campaign. And if blue-chip multinational companies such as Marks & Spencer deliberately embellish their product descriptions then they do this for good reason: namely, that it sells!

While this may sound like an unrelated example, it is in fact highly significant because your CV is effectively a sales document and every time you send off your CV you are trying to sell yourself to employers. Just as Marks & Spencer are competing in a highly competitive sector (retail), the job market is no less competitive. So if a leading company like Marks & Spencer recognises the value of embellishment to boost sales it is worthwhile bearing this in mind when you come to sell yourself on your own CV.

That said, you do need some balance. The language you use needs to be appropriate for the level and job you are targeting. In addition, you are not writing a novel so there is no need to try to out-do Wordsworth on the lyricism front. If you can just tell the employer you possess the skills, qualities and experience he or she is looking for in sharp, punchy, proactive terms then you are effectively taking your first steps towards interview. This is because what you are doing is starting the all-important transition from *telling* to *selling*.

Okay, I realise that CVs are not the same as menus, and I freely admit that selling to employers is quite different from selling foodstuffs to consumers, but despite this the fact remains that selling is selling, and if you can somehow dress something (or someone) up so that it (or they) sound(s) more interesting and appealing then this is only going to improve the chances of a sale.

Without further ado let us contemplate this using some examples.

Quite often office/administrative sector workers write sentences such as these:

- Handled client calls

- Entered data into a database

- Dealt with correspondence

In the general scheme of things there is nothing wrong with sentences such as those listed above. They are grammatically correct, they are relevant, and in all probability they are an accurate reflection of duties undertaken by the candidate in the course of their daily work.

Nevertheless, the sentences are short, basic and rather passive. They are also taking up three whole lines to say very little. Moreover, when you examine what they are actually saying it is nothing special, and certainly is not anything over and above what at least half the other candidates will be saying. In other words they are *'quiche and salad'* phrases as opposed to *'This is not just food, this is M&S food'*. I would wager that many employers would not give CVs like this a second glance, especially if you consider that the majority of the other CVs piled on their desk are almost certainly bound to be better.

So what can we do to improve things?

You may have some factual entries along these lines on your own CV. If so, please highlight one of them now, and we can try a useful exercise.

Hands-on session

Before I explain just how I would go about things, it would be useful if you could take your own CV and have a go at improving the basic sentence you have highlighted. Try to make it more appealing to employers while remembering to keep it relatively concise.

Do you want to spend the rest of your life selling sugared water or do you want the chance to change the world? THE LINE STEVE JOBS USED TO LURE JOHN SCULLEY AS APPLE'S CEO

Okay, let's assume you have had a go at improving your own sentence (I'm very trusting, if not naively optimistic). Now let's go back to the original sentences and consider them further.

The first thing we should do is delve deeper into the bones of the sentences to see just what the message is and how it is being transmitted. If you do this you will see that at the most basic level all the sentences are doing is saying '*I did this*' and '*I did that*'. No more, no less. Effectively they are just *telling*.

This would be all well and good if everyone else was just telling. However, as you should be aware by now, at least some of the candidates you will be competing against will not only be *telling*, some will also be *selling*.

What are you doing in your sentence? '*Telling*' or '*Selling*'?

To make the transition the first thing you really need to do is to coax out the literary Del Boy Trotter salesperson in you and bring those verbs, adverbs, nouns and adjectives to market. You know it makes sense!

One of the first things we can do is identify words and phrases which can make us sound more proactive. In this instance '*handled*', '*entered*' and '*dealt with*' are phrases which, although not strictly speaking passive, are nonetheless not particularly proactive either. So, our first task is to improve these words. We can do this thus:

- Managed client calls
- Managed data entry
- Managed correspondence

These sentences are now a bit more proactive, primarily because of the use of a more powerful word *managed*. It's a better all-round word because among other things it has connotations with more responsibility, more organisation and even a more complete job. Nevertheless, the sentences still need improving. For starters, the fact that they are basic and take up three lines to say very little still holds true. On top of this, they now look repetitive and unimaginative. This is where it helps if you can unleash your creative talents. On the negative side, some people are far more creative than others, and if you are not particularly creative you may struggle with this. On the plus side, you don't necessarily have to go down one single fixed path. You should remember that there is frequently a variety of different routes and options you can take to make improvements. Sometimes it is not vital *exactly* which path you take, as long as you reach your ultimate goal of making improvements, and making the sentence far more interesting, relevant and proactive.

For example, you could say something like this:

- Entrusted to liaise with important clients by telephone
- Ensured accurate database data entry
- Managed a variety of correspondence including letters and faxes

How do these changes compare to your new sentence?

The sentences above show further improvements on a variety of levels. The most obvious one is that there is now more to each of them, in terms of words, meaning and effect. They are also using proactive terms, and a bit of variety has been introduced which in turn helps maintain interest.

I would say that if you improved the original sentences to ones such as these then the chances of you getting noticed by the employer would certainly increase, although perhaps not enough to land an interview. After all, although the sentences are better, they are still not particularly striking. They could all be improved in global terms for starters, but in addition, once you get in depth, cracks become apparent. For example, it doesn't sound eloquent to say *'database data'* or *'variety of correspondence'*. A bit more embellishment and refinement is therefore required.

And what about your sentence(s)? Could it (or they) use more embellishment? If so, have a go at making further improvements before reading on.

How wonderful it is that nobody need wait a single moment before starting to improve the world.
DIARY OF A YOUNG GIRL (ANNE FRANK)

Going back to our examples, we could say this:

- Orchestrated communications with important clients

- Consistently updated and managed the office database

- In charge of managing important correspondence including letters, faxes and emails

Among other things, here we are introducing extra elements to substantiate the sentences and further heighten the achievement. For example, *orchestrating communications* is more evocative, proactive and ultimately more impressive than just *liaising* with clients. Similarly, the second sentence has been improved not only by adding an extra element to the data management aspect, but also by introducing the concept of time and more precisely the candidate's ability not only to perform a task once, but frequently, over a greater period of time. In addition to this, the third sentence also ramps up the position of responsibility aspect by incorporating the term *'in charge of'*. Phrases like this are useful because they can help boost the perception that you aren't just a typical run-of-the-mill worker who can do an average job, but are actually someone on a higher plane: a doer, a go-getter, an achiever.

Obviously, one little phrase alone isn't going to cement this message or provoke the employer to dash over to your house with a contract. However, if you introduce more and more proactive terms, phrases and sales points then these start to add up, and just like adding weights to scales, if you keep on adding them then this can eventually be enough to tip the balance. Certainly, the addition of relevant and impressive achievements to your CV usually serves to add weight to your application.

Of course you cannot use terms like *'in charge of'* if this isn't true. However, you do have some creative licence. For example, if you are the only one in your office who deals with phone calls, and your boss trusts you to take care of them, then effectively you are in charge of answering phone calls regardless of whether it says this on your job badge or not. In which case it makes sense to take advantage of this fact and flaunt it! Some people miss some great opportunities to sell themselves on their CV simply because they restrict themselves to terminology used on their job description rather than taking a step back and writing about what they do in unashamed proactive terms.

Look back at your own sentence and ask yourself whether or not you can use a bit of creative licence to bolster the impression that you are an achiever. Have a try at altering it, and do it now before reading further.

Any activity becomes creative when the doer cares about doing it right, or better. JOHN UPDIKE

How is your sentence coming along? Is it better than before?

Returning to our examples; there is no particular set path that you have to take to improve things, so just off the top of my head we could say:

- Orchestrated internal/external communications with important clients and key stakeholders

- Consistently ensured 100 per cent accurate management of the company CRM database

- In complete charge of a broad range of office management functions including documentation and correspondence.

Again, these new amendments add an extra dimension to the sentences. For example, they are now not only more informative, but are also more specific, relevant and ultimately more impressive. Additionally, they also introduce new keywords such as *internal/ external, stakeholders, CRM, office management* and *documentation*. While it isn't strictly necessary to do this, the net effect is potentially to tick one or two more boxes on the employer's wish list. All in all this helps portray the candidate as a more versatile professional with a broader range of relevant skills.

As we can see, the candidate has gone from being perceived as someone who *did a bit of this and did a bit of that* to someone who is demonstrating that they are far more versatile, have more strings to their bow, and can actually do a far better job. In short, they have gone from someone who merely carries out data entry duties to someone who successfully manages the company CRM database with 100 per cent accuracy. Do you see the difference? If you can, employers can too. This is why writing proactively works, and is why it gets results for those who can do it well.

If your CV isn't doing you justice, then writing positively, concisely and proactively should go some way to help redress the balance.

Of course, this is easier said than done, so if you want some practice and a further insight into just what is involved then I have included below examples taken from real CVs. Whenever we write CVs professionally the CV goes through various stages, including refining the sentences down while making them more proactive. The examples below include client original sentences, suggestions from my trainees, and comments from myself. I should also point out these trainees have degrees, a writing background and were the cream of the crop in initial tests – 99 per cent of applicants (including applications from professional CV writers) didn't get this far.

Organised and managed construction, deconstruction and manning of an exhibition stand at venues such as London's Earls Court

Trainee: *Successfully organised and managed all logistics for an exhibition stand at venues such as London's Earls Court*

Me: Half of this is redundant, and overall it is not proactive enough. However, if you fixed the redundancy aspect then this will give you more space to make it more proactive. For example you could say something along these lines:

> *Organised and managed logistics and staffing of popular trade stands at major international exhibitions*

Managed a team responsible for accurate aircraft engine data assessment, work package generation and rescheduling future periodic servicings

Trainee: *Managed servicing schedules and aircraft data assessments continually improving workflow efficiency*

Me: More concise but you need to remember to double-check logic. 'continually improving workflow efficiency' isn't feasible. There is a point where it is finite.

Trainee: *Managed servicing schedules, aircraft data assessments and teams to successfully improve workflow efficiency*

Embrace promotional and seasonal changes with profits in mind

Trainee: *Identified key strategies to boost profits by successfully capitalising on promotional and seasonal products*

Me: This is a bit over the top and somewhat muddled up. You could keep the same sort of things but put them in a different order and it would be much better.

Trainee: *Identified key strategies, successfully capitalising on promotional and seasonal products to boost profits*

Me: This is an improvement but it's somewhat over the top still.

Trainee: *Identified and successfully capitalised on trends to promote seasonal products and boost profits*

Successfully managed external communication agencies to ensure a clear company strategy was developed and the portfolio brands were maximised. This includes crisis management planning

Trainee: *Forged strong relations with communication agencies, to develop a corporate strategy and maximise portfolio brands*

Me: The sentence could be good but falls down primarily by your use of one word 'to' which arguably renders the sentence illogical.

Trainee: *Forged strong relations with communication agencies, developing corporate strategy and maximising portfolio brands*

Managed a team responsible for Sales, Marketing, Applications, Research and development (approximately 80 people)

Trainee: *Personally managed a marketing team of 80 including sales and research, to achieve a focus for quality and service*

Me: The sentence lacks a natural flow.

Trainee: *Personally managed a team of 80, maximising performance across sales, marketing, research and development*

Me: This is much better, and you have achieved it purely by concentrating on something far less complicated.

✓ Writing flexibly

Let us not be too particular; it is better to have old second-hand diamonds than none at all. MARK TWAIN

... this may come as a surprise to some people, but a CV is a dynamic document. This section gives you important insights into how writing flexibly can help you achieve better results in the job market ...

If you have seen the TV series *Little Britain* you may be familiar with the shop sketches involving a fusspot customer called Mr Mann and a much maligned shopkeeper. Essentially, the sketches revolve around Mr Mann asking for something perfectly natural, but then somehow managing to exasperate the unfortunate shopkeeper by insisting on all kinds of weird extras, conditions and provisos, such as a date with a woman with a glass eye, a painting of an irked (not vexed) kitten and a James Last record with sleeve notes specifically written by Dr Graeme Garden. Little wonder then that the shop-keeper hardly makes a sale!

This (albeit unusual) example illustrates that if you are too rigid and too pernickety about everything then you risk missing out on what you are looking for. Indeed, just as Mr Mann missed out on games, magazines and the woman of his dreams due to his stubbornness, you too could also miss out on your dream job if you are too rigid and fail to exercise a degree of flexibility in your CV writing.

Let's put it another way. Imagine for example that you had a shop, let's say a sports shop, and you stocked just one item, let's say pink XL size rugby shorts. How many do you think you would sell per 100 customers?

I think I don't have to tell you that the answer is probably not many! And why? Because you are being too restrictive, and not considering your customers.

Just as it sounds crazy that someone would try selling only one item to a large cross-section of sports shop customers, it is equally crazy when job seekers think they can sell themselves to a wide cross-section of employers with one immovable, cast-iron CV. However, this is what thousands of job seekers do every single day, and this is why many of them do not succeed in their applications. For the best results you need to consider your customer (i.e. the employer) and be flexible enough to sell him or her what he or she is looking for. Yes, I know that this is a bit of a drag and it is not particularly easy, but on the other hand it isn't an impossible pipe dream either. In fact, in many cases it is highly realistic. And best of all, you don't even need to go out and get a glass eye, because – guess what? – while employers do look for the best candidate, most are not looking for the weird and wonderful, but just someone who can do a good honest job for them. A lot of the time this isn't too much to ask; numerous candidates could easily do the one job on offer. However, if ten candidates all have good credentials for a particular job, but only one of them really manages to tell the employer on their CV exactly what he or she is looking for then there are no prizes for guessing who will get the job!

So how do you find out what the employer is looking for? And how do you include this on your CV?

Actually, this isn't rocket science. Most employers will pretty much tell you what they are looking for either in the job specification or in the advertisement. Even if they don't, you can always be resourceful and look at similar advertisements or job specifications and find out what similar employers are looking for. Obviously, this isn't quite as good, because they may be looking for slightly different things, but usually if you look at job specifications for very similar jobs then at the very least there will be overlaps, and this should give you something to work with.

So how do you include this on your CV? Again, with flexibility.

Let us take the example of a senior manager now wanting to downscale to the post of PA. This kind of thing isn't so unusual and probably happens more than most people realise.

The CV below comes from a client who had been trying to downscale without success. As you can see, she had been applying for PA jobs with a CV which reflected her previous (senior managerial) employment, rather than focusing on the new job she wanted to target. In effect, she had been trying to bang a round peg in a square hole. After all, employers looking for PAs actually want a PA; they don't want a senior office manager, a data entry clerk or a dustman.

In addition to focusing on the wrong target, the original CV was also cluttered and too long (it is still too long now – even after I subsequently cut it down by half for the sake of this book).

To protect privacy, I have changed the details.

22 York Road
Leeds
LS31 9UN
Mobile: 07700 900315
Email: sandra67@gmail.com

Sandra Lockwood BA (Hons)

Profile:
A dynamic and adaptable senior business professional with a track record in the commercial environment across logistics, supply chain and global FMCG Industries. Has held a number of very senior strategic and operational roles with experience of leading teams on large and complex projects both in the UK and the EU.

Key Skills:
- Leading and developing strategy
- Financial management expertise
- Problem solving
- Project management
- Developing work environments based on collaboration and trust.

Career History:
2006–Present
ABC Ltd

2007–2012   Senior Development Manager
- Leadership of Development teams across all trade channels, with the remit to build ABC's position in the trade as a category expert internationally.
- Travelling and working with directors and other staff on trade shows.
- Creating and enforcing day to day operational strategy across drivers for commercial team across all UK and European channels to ensure the delivery of annual plans for operations and strategy.
- Accountable for management of all commercial investment policies including outlining of promotional strategies and international trade execution.
- Delivering a refreshed Category strategy for execution across internal and external customer base, with lead development of Financial profitability stages.

Key Achievements:
- Developed new approaches to promotional understanding and application – involving developing internal and external data and new guidelines relevant to current customer challenges.
- Delivery of Category Thought Leadership to re-frame the trade perspective of ABC throughout the organisation.
- Created and implemented a suite of automated online tools to track and manage business KPIs including NPS and market share.
- Developed and launched new integrated customer planning processes to help plan and deliver annual benefits of approx £100k.
- Launched and developed a companywide Category Strategy in the UK and designed and executed HR development programmes across Europe.

▶

- Successful streamlining of process to eliminate unnecessary meetings and duplication of work to allow more added value contribution to business.

2006–2007   Development Manager
- To manage effective internal operations and 100 staff on a day to day basis including pre defined initiatives which ensure the delivery of key business targets.
- To manage the effective delivery of business goals into the market place by executing multichannel category initiatives based commercial propositions and the required toolkit to facilitate the delivery of commercial objectives.
- To lead and manage internal process alignment of business priorities and key marketing initiatives thus ensuring commitment to deliver the strategic and operational plan.
- To identify commercial opportunities and provide data led arguments which deliver financial and strategic objectives whilst providing Customers with incremental growth opportunities.
- To lead management processes which set out the prioritization of the portfolio to the UK commercial organisation and which facilitate Category growth for consumers both in the UK and EU.
- To deliver the annual workbook to provide the commercial team with the context and guidance on range, distribution and launch activities for NPD/Range extensions, to enable a timely and accurate annual planning process to take place.
- To lead and organize commercial conferences and events in Blackpool and Stuttgart.
- To provide visible tracking of key initiatives to understand, analyse and report on the category impact, customer and business benefits.

Key Achievements:
- Led Project Teams to deliver new events resulting in store activation in over 300 stores. Delivering over £3m profits in year 1 of launch.
- Developed a new process to ensure complete Sales toolkits delivered 16 weeks prior to launch. This resulted in an improved listing rate for 2006 and 2007 in the UK and was then implemented as best practice approach across Europe.
- Led a project team in Germany to identify best practice approach for managing process to minimize write off costs, delivering annual savings of £1m in 2006.

2004–2005   Marketing Manager   DEF Ltd

- Responsible for purchase initiatives and activation within multiple channels resulting in increased distribution and higher sales values.
- Developed sector specific strategies including the development of promotional targets to ensure effective profitable sales growth.
- Executed category management analysis – creating and reporting on category solutions across different retail customers.
- Led sales planning processes to ensure brand growth for implementation plans as agreed with the marketing director.
- Liaised with the marketing director and worked with the teams researching solutions specifically for agreed channels.

Key Achievements:
- Developed retail store plans, and provided account manager guidance incorporating POS drivers to educate the Sales team and drive in-store presence.
- Successfully provided high quality business reviews, category and consumers insights resulting in incremental sales benefits.
- Provided business plans for various channels including the development of a range of specific FMCG products.

2001–2004	**Business Development Manager**	**GGG Ltd**

- Strategic and operational responsibility, including marketing, business development, client and supplier relationships, and financial reporting.
- Responsible for line management, team development and training.

Key Achievements:
- Successfully managed a project team in enabling the business to expand into new markets through development of a new business start up.
- Designed and implemented new customer service protocol; responsible for an improvement in client satisfaction and sales.
- Analysis and review of the supplier base resulted in detailed streamlining.
- Worked with senior managers to achieve migration to the new Manchester office on schedule and without incident.

2000	**Manager**	**HJK Ltd**

- Manager of a small print shop in charge of all day to day activities.
- Responsible for line management, team development, training, accounts, reports, correspondence, marketing and administration.

Education & Qualifications:

1991 – 1995	BSc (Hons) Business Administration	Glasgow University
1983 – 1990	3 A levels and 9 GCSEs	Glasgow College

As you can see, it is in no way, shape or form a PA CV. There is a bit of a catch-22 situation here. If you have never worked as a specialist PA, but the employer is looking for a PA as opposed to a senior manager, an account manager, a data entry clerk or a secretary, what can you do?

Well, what you can't do is be static, inflexible and naive enough to just apply with a CV which doesn't address the job properly. Instead you have to be flexible, creative and proactive.

If this lady had worked as a PA all her career then she could have just submitted a specialist PA CV. However, this wasn't the case, and so more thought, consideration and creativity were needed.

What we could (and did) do was look at all the many strings to her bow, ask her about her (more relevant) experience not already mentioned on the CV, and accentuate all her PA-related skills and traits, while giving the less relevant experience a much lower profile. So, for example, on her profile, rather than talking about business and management skills we instead highlighted more relevant skills which she possessed such as *judgement, initiative* and *client relations*. (And we identified these as being relevant to her target job from the job specification she sent us.) Additionally, whereas her previous CV had given almost equal weighting to all her previous roles, this time the more relevant roles were given more weighting, and the less relevant were given less weighting, or were excluded altogether.

It is a bit unnatural and goes against the grain to do this to some degree, and what you are effectively doing is playing some of your base cards instead of the face and trump cards. But as mentioned, it is often a matter of horses for courses, and you sometimes need to be open-minded, lucid and adaptable if you are to win the hand (or in this case, post).

As it turns out, this lady had plenty of skills in her repertoire to make a first-class PA. In addition to working closely with directors (effectively, a PA role without the title), she showed that she was an excellent organiser and could clearly work on her own initiative, she had vast senior-level meeting experience, together with excellent communication, presentation and relation-building skills. In addition to this she knew the sector she worked in inside out, and if that wasn't enough she had first-class administration skills. All in all she had plenty of strong credentials; it was just a matter of bringing these credentials to the fore rather than burying them in the detail.

As mentioned in the *CV writing myths* chapter of the book, people often make the mistake of thinking that they need to separate out each job, and write in detail about each and every job. This is all well and good if each job is relevant to the job that you are targeting. However, this isn't always the case. In fact, it often isn't the case. Consequently, if you follow a rigid structure, you risk trying to sell the customer (i.e. the employer) something he or she doesn't really want. In the case of this lady she was originally trying to sell the employer a senior manager/marketing manager/business development specialist when all he really wanted was a PA. By writing flexibly and creatively this lady was subsequently able to sell herself as a PA to potential employers.

Without writing flexibly this just wouldn't have been possible.

Please see the one-page version of the more PA-focused CV overleaf. I say 'version', because, to protect the client's privacy, it has been altered in this book. I have changed personal/work details, dates and have also excluded some specifics.

Sandra Lockwood

♦ 22 York Road, Leeds LS31 9UN ♦ 07700 900315 ♦ sandra67@gmail.com

PERSONAL PROFILE

A reliable, motivated and dynamic PA/Manager with initiative, a degree in Business Administration and a proven record ensuring first-class office management, client relations and MD support

CAREER & ACHIEVEMENTS TO DATE

PA/Manager   2000–date
ABC Ltd (2006–date) | DEF Ltd (2005) | GGG Ltd (2001–2004) | HJK Ltd (2000)

KEY ACHIEVEMENTS

♦ Handpicked by *ABC*'s MD to assist him develop important projects and initiatives (2006–date)
♦ Organised board meetings, kept minutes and built client relations at top-level in the UK & Europe
♦ Attended trade shows and conferences in the UK and Europe with the MD, helping with networking
♦ Selected by the MD to represent him at key European sites, overseeing HR development processes
♦ Organised and successfully managed successful conferences and events in the UK and Germany
♦ Oversaw departments to ensure impeccable finances and first-class business administration
♦ Reorganised and streamlined office policies and automated IT procedures to increase efficiency
♦ Commended by the MD for improving customer planning processes to deliver £100,000 in benefits
♦ Awarded a £25,000 bonus by the MD for outstanding contribution to *ABC*'s record profits in 2012
♦ Worked with *DEF*'s marketing director and liaised with teams to ensure channel success (2005)
♦ Ensured 100% accurate category solution reporting for a cross section of retail customers
♦ Assisted and supported the *GGG*'s COO to achieve a major site migration to remit (2001–2004)
♦ Managed supplier selection, budgets and purchasing to fit out and launch the new office on time
♦ Ensured first-class office administration, data management, reports and accounts for *HJK* (2000)

QUALIFICATIONS & PERSONAL DETAILS

D.O.B. 22nd Jan 1978   *Health: In Excellent Health*   *Nationality: British*

BSc (Hons) in Business Administration, Glasgow University   1999

SKILLS & KEY COMPETENCIES

♦ Proven experience supporting MDs
♦ Excellent PA and organisational skills
♦ Hands-on IT and administration expertise
♦ Proven client/stakeholder relations skills
♦ Outstanding people/communication skills

♦ Confident and committed team player
♦ Highly efficient, pragmatic and reliable
♦ Shrewd judge and decision maker
♦ Natural drive, dedication and initiative
♦ Professional, tactful and diplomatic

INTERESTS & REFERENCES

Interests: Cooking, Opera, Dance | References available on request

As you can see, by being open and creative you can make a huge difference to your CV, and applications as a whole. Moreover, you need to think about at least flexibly tweaking whenever you apply for a new job. Contrary to what some people may believe there is no such thing as an effective multi-purpose, one-serves-all CV. Yes, some people do try to use one CV for all their applications. However, this isn't the best way forward (as they usually find out to their cost).

It is often a matter of horses for courses.

The way you sell yourself for one job often needs to be different from the way you sell yourself for another job (and, as you know, your CV is effectively a sales tool).

One analogy which springs to mind is one key and ten locks: you may be able to open one of the locks with the one key. However, if you want to open the most locks, then you need the right key for each of them. And each key is usually different.

Remember, a CV is a dynamic document which not only can change, but which actually should change depending upon the job in question.

For example, many PA job specifications mention things like 'diary management', 'typing ability', 'secretarial skills' etc. However, this lady's target job didn't mention any of those things in the job specification, so instead we concentrated on telling the employer what they wanted to hear, and included keywords from that particular job specification. If it had mentioned things such as 'organising trips for directors', we would have asked the client if she had experience in that, and if so we would have included that.

The above section illustrates writing flexibly in a nutshell. But reading about it and actually doing it for yourself are two separate things; just as with pretty much every other aspect of CV writing there is far more to it than meets the eye, and a lot of it comes with experience.

Elsewhere in the book I have described writing CVs to job specifications and other methods of writing flexibly such as combining jobs, and being flexible about placement of entries and indeed inclusion (or omission) of whole sections (see Adapting to adaptability – job specifications in Chapter 4). As a matter of fact, writing flexibly is like a lot of other creative subjects in that the possibilities and permutations are almost endless. The main rule to remember is essentially this: if your CV tells the employer the things he or she wants to hear and it does this in a neat, compact, proactive and highly relevant manner then you are on the right track. If you put yourself in the shoes of the employer and realise that in the employer's eyes your CV isn't appealing, focused, or doesn't sell you enough for the job in question then there is something wrong. Following rigid guidelines or CV myths will almost certainly worsen not solve the situation, but if you write flexibly, concisely and proactively then this can be the tonic you need to help you get back on track.

8

CV-speak – laying it out

'Tis better to be silent and be thought a fool, than to speak and remove all doubt. ABRAHAM LINCOLN (ATTRIBUTED)

... how to view your CV from other perspectives – after all, it's not you who will be reading it ...

Hopefully you will already have learned lots of useful things in this book, and your CV-writing skills will be slicker, sharper and more finely tuned than ever before. But before we say *'see thee'* to CVs, I thought I'd add a fun section, first to check that you've been listening, and secondly so you can see for yourself just how much you have (or haven't) been taking in.

Please join in – it's for you after all.

CV ESP

If only my CV could speak to me ...

Well in this exercise it can!

I want you to get into CV ESP mode and imagine that your CV is trying to tell you something – maybe big important clues about what is wrong, what could be better – or both.

I've included some thought bubbles to prompt your thinking (or even fill in if you are feeling inspired).

If you've read the book this far you probably won't be too surprised to hear that I won't be sitting here tutting if you just write one or two bullet points rather than ten-page essays, and I won't come chasing you down the road with a cane if you haven't copied my suggestions verbatim – there is more than one way to skin a cat. And, as I hope you will know by now, you need to be open-minded, flexible and think for yourself if you want to write a great CV. It's your *own* noggin you need to use, not anyone else's. And if you try the painting-by-numbers approach to CV writing, as other books encourage, then you'll just end up with something standard, bog-standard or bog-destined – and we wouldn't want that!

So, please, just sit down, get a pencil out and have a go. It's a bit of fun, but there is a serious side too, as you'll get an idea of just how far you've come.

CV ESP EXAMPLE 1

This example is an amended one-page résumé, sent to me by a US client. I've changed the personal details and a few other things, but it's pretty much his original in terms of the message and how it was laid out.

Your job is to get in tune with the CV, listen to what it has to say, then think about (or fill in) the thought bubbles associated with various sections. Go on: help this CV express itself.

Jim Groves

690 Maple Ave
Stockton
CA 23083
444-342-4561
jim72@jimg.com

OBJECTIVE
A senior level position within a leading media company

EXPERIENCE

8/2012–Present
Senior Copy Writer and Production Specialist
ABC Network
Media, PA
Senior Copy Writer and Production Director for a major news organization, responsible for a number of roles and tasks including creative writing, editing and proofing copy, design (including advising on website design) and all aspects of studio production, including hands-on experience with audio editing techniques and all audio engineering duties. Including 5 years' experience managing all aspects of creative process management; creating the creative brief, selecting and hiring copy writers, casting, recruiting and scheduling talent, and ensuring the project is delivered in accordance with network directives and completed to meet all deadlines. Some of my work has been chosen for national TV and radio campaigns and I have also been seconded to third party companies on a short-term contract basis. Additionally I have helped in creating new promotional campaigns for both TV and radio for major clients like Disney, Pepsi, and KFC. Amongst other things I am responsible for a considerable increase in the picture/photo library, and I also helped upgrade our studio capabilities in LA. To this aim I created the configuration to eliminate studio and production flaws and also contributed ideas on the design of new studios. Things like label designs have greatly enhanced our professional presentation, and especially on the West coast.

Previous posts (1997–2012) include Board Operator and engineering assistant

EDUCATION
Miami University, 1994 Bachelor's Degree in Media Communications.

SKILLS
MS Excel
MS Word
MS Access
Pro Tools.
Adobe Audition
Cool Edit Pro
AudioVault

INTERESTS
Baseball, swimming, running, movies

Here is a bigger bubble for you to say a bit more about the CV in general.

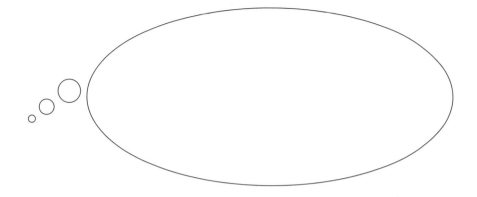

CV ESP EXAMPLE 2

This is an amended IT CV sent to me by an IT sector client. I've changed details and cut the document down by a full page. Again please fill in the speech bubbles.

PETER R JAMES

22 Station Lane, Middlesbrough, North Yorks TS2 3YY
Tel: 01632 960411
Email: pjr80@pjr.com

PROFILE

Seasoned IT professional with diverse technical expertise and comprehensive experience in many IT areas including implementations of technologies, application of cutting-edge technologies, managing projects relating to technical, functional and operational guidelines. Abilities and experience include programming, coding, business analysis, consultancy, process optimisation, database design, standards, working with off-shore teams and delivering international project rollouts.

- Many years experience of ITIL/ITSM processes
- Experience in System Analysis, Design and Development in Axway Synchrony Gateway Interchange
- Advanced EDI, XML, IBM WTX knowledge
- Have used numerous adapters to send EDI documents across different platforms using diverse set of protocols, viz. FTP, SFTP, HTTP, HTTPS, AS2
- Experience in Interface development, Business processes, Mapping, Gap Analysis Technical Development. Functional analysis and Configuration
- EAI & EDI solutions, Design and Administration, multi-tier architecture
- Technical skills on IBM WebSphere Transformation Extender, IBM WebSphere MQ and EDI standards
- Configuration, Space management, Capacity Planning, and customisation of WTX in the AIX environment
- Internal and external 3rd party support experience internationally
- Domain expertise including Supply Chain Logistics and Warehouse Management
- ANSI X12, EDIFACT, GS1, OAGIS BOD, IDOC and bespoke formats
- Application maintenance, troubleshooting, production support and bug fixing experience

SKILLS

- ◆ Protocols: SOAP, SSL/SSH, WebServices, FTP, SFTP, HTTP, AS/2, SMTP, TELNET
- ◆ RDBMS: Oracle 9i
- ◆ Integration: IBM Tivoli, IBM WebSphere Transformation Extender 8.2, IBM WebSphere DataStage TX 8.0 (aka. Mercator/Ascential), IBM WebSphere Message Broker, IBM WebSphere Message Queue, Oracle AQ, Axway Synchrony Gateway Interchange (Cyclone)
- ◆ EDI Standards: EDIFACT, ANSI X12, IDOCS, TRADACOM, RosettaNet, ebxml, OAGIS BODs
- ◆ Business Apps: OTM 5.7
- ◆ Languages: Java, J2EE, VB
- ◆ Web: CSS, XML, HTML, XHTML
- ◆ OS: Unix, Linux,  Windows 9X/NT/2000/XP, AIX
- ◆ Project Mgt. MS Project

EDUCATION

- ◆ Bachelor of Science in Computer Technology 1994–1997, York University
- ◆ Fundamentals, Map Designer, Database Interface Designer, Adapters (Database, HTTP, FTP), Event Server and Integration Flow Designer, FORTRAN, Pascal, Oracle

---

PROFESSIONAL EXPERIENCE

ABC UK Ltd *Feb 2010 to date*

ABC is a leader in the world of IT services with 322 offices worldwide and an annual turnover of over £1 billion

IT Consultant
Responsible for providing IT solutions for SCi applications using OTM
Environment: IBM WebSphere MQ V6.2, OTM V5.6
Client: FG Global

Key Accomplishments:

- Implemented an Integration Gateway for the SCi application via IBM WebSphere MQ implementation with a flow of messages to and from the application.

- Responsible for preparing the Solution Design Specification documents and Business Requirements Specification.
- Worked with first/second/third line support to deliver WMS migration.
- Gap Analysis Report analysis of both Source and Destination, identifying mandatory fields and the business logics to be implemented.
- Drafted the Mapping Specification documents for business flows related to the integration and delivery of the new WMS system.
- Prepared Unit Test Plan & Unit Test Results Documentation and liaised with QA on both development and client testing environments.
- Assisted support with the resolution of assorted technical issues.
- Prepared the Business Requirement Specification Document and the Solution Design Document.
- Prepared the Mapping Specification documents for the business flows involved between the Management Systems, Integration Layer and SCi application.

XYZ PLC (formerly Cambridge Solutions UK Ltd)   *May 2004 to Feb 2010*

XYZ is an IT Solutions company to clients
across multiple industries.

Analyst

Managed projects and technical aspects; this involved the design and delivery of requirements on system design, new technologies, performance/process optimisation. It also involved technology and platform analysis. Accountable for feasibility analysis, KPI's, risks, technical infrastructure, customer environment modelling, project evaluations, UAT and rollout.

Environment: Axway Synchrony Gateway Interchange, IBM WebSphere WTX V8.2, IBM WebSphere MQ V6.0

Client: FEG PLC

Key Accomplishments:

- Planning Requirement Analysis, Client Interaction, Design, Coding, Testing, Support and Documentation.
- Gathering and documenting User Requirements, Requirement Analysis, converting requirements into High Level Design Documents.

- Gap Analysis Report analysis of field attributes of both Source and Destination, identifying the mandatory fields and the business logics to be implemented.
- Message Interface Guidelines documentation for ANSI X12, EDIFACT, OAGIS BODs standards.
- Created Type Trees and Maps.
- Multi-part logic framework design and implementation.
- Business data exchange with client systems.
- Unit Test Planning & Unit Test Results Documentation.
- Hub Integration testing & QA.
- Review maps development and tuning.
- Deployment of the objects & configuration of the flows in the production environment.
- Mentoring Franchise analysts on Standards, Processes and Guidelines.
- Liaison with Franchise Analyst team/client and related solution providers to make sure project meets all specifications.
- 24/7 production support.

Other Programs/Platforms
- ♦ Mento MS Windows server 2003, SQL DB & Vmware ESX server, wireless networks, managed VLAN, Windows NT4/3.11 to Windows XP/2003 server environment, 3Ds Max scripting algorithms, Windows server administration using *Distributed Bucket Computing* algorithms, standards including *EDIFACT*, *ANSI X12* and *OAGIS BODs*, Pascal, C, C ++ language, FTP, SFTP, HTTP, HTTPS, AS2, AOD tools, object orientated design methods, Access and Excel

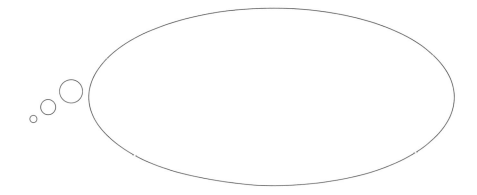

CV ESP EXAMPLE 3

The last example is a CV that was sent to me by someone looking for administration management work. Again I have changed the details.

Jane Weeks
76 Elm Grove, AB12 2NR
Jw122@gmail.com
07700 900432

- -

Personal Summary
I am a good listener
I am supportive of others
I have a good sense of humour
I am intelligent
I work well autonomously or in a team
I learn quickly
I have a 'can do' attitude
I share my knowledge to empower others
I am flexible
I am friendly
I am well read
I am funny
I am pragmatic
I am proactive and assertive
I am a good communicator
I am able to prioritise my work load to meet deadlines

Education and Qualifications

Sep 2003–July 2006   Graduate of Aberdeen University (History)

Skills gained:
- Group work (including projects) and working independently
- Reports and working to deadlines
- Research of a variety of subjects

2001–July 2003 – Access to University Course, Aberdeen University

Employment History, Key Duties, Skills and Achievements

2006–Present: Administrator, ABC Ltd.

Duties:
- Assisting the managers and senior staff
- Secretarial and IT support
- Managing and overseeing office procedures
- Assisting with the recruitment
- Updating databases

Skills gained:
- Gaining more knowledge on administration procedures
- Building on my team working skills
- Enhancing my typing skills

Achievements:
- Successfully trained new staff
- Assisted at several meetings

Apr 2006 – 6 weeks work experience in a cake factory office.

2004–2006: Various temporary administrative positions during my studies including Receptionist at the Hilton Hotel, Aberdeen

97–Jul 03: Personal Assistant, SDF Ltd, Perth

Duties:
- Diary management and professional and personal support for the M.D.
- Scheduling to deadlines
- Booking international travel and schedules
- Coordinating database and Excel updates
- Recruiting cleaning staff

Skills gained:
- The ability to work to inflexible deadlines
- Multitasking
- Experience of managing junior staff members
- Attention to detail

Achievements:
- Project managing the purchasing and installation of 7 new PCs

95–97: Receptionist – HDS Ltd, Perth

Duties:
- Answering all incoming calls for staff and forwarding messages
- Managing front of house on a rota basis

Skills gained:
- Tact and diplomacy

94–95:   Telephonist – HDS Ltd, Perth

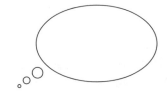

Duties:
- Answering incoming calls
- Booking meeting rooms

Skills gained:
- Developing a professional telephone manner

Office Skills
- Miscrosoft Word, Excel, Powerpoint and Outlook
- 65 WPM
- Photocopying, scanners and faxes

Hobbies
- Music, travelling, cinema
- Currently writing some short stories and poetry

References

Mr Jim Kelsey	Mr Jon Hume
Manager	Manager
ABC Ltd	DEF Ltd
Aberdeen AB1 2JK	Perth PH7 2UY

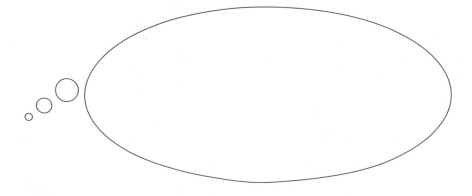

I hope you will have not only had a go at that, but also found it much easier going than if you hadn't read the rest of the book. Maybe you will have different answers from mine; if so that's perfectly fine as long as your answers are rational, logical and make sense. All three CVs could be greatly improved, and I haven't given the poor CVs much room to express themselves (via ESP to you) in the speech bubbles, so there are plenty of things/issues still left unsaid. Even so, hopefully this section will still serve as a good exercise to help you when it comes to assuming the *CV mode position* and getting in tune with your own curriculum vitae.

With that, let's have a look at what these CVs may be saying (or in some cases screaming out!).

COME IN CV NUMBER 1, RECEIVING ...

Jim Groves

690 Maple Ave

Stockton

CA 23083

444-342-4561

jim72@jimg.com

Yeah, yeah I know all that!

Fine, but I'd rather you talk more about me, rather than where I live

OBJECTIVE
A senior level position within a leading media company

EXPERIENCE

Ooh, I feel somewhat out of kilter. That's quite a mouthful, and what is it I was supposed to be doing before 2012?

8/2012–Present
Senior Copy Writer and Production Specialist
ABC Network
Media, PA
Senior Copy Writer and Production Director for a major news organization, responsible for a number of roles and tasks including creative writing, editing and proofing copy, design (including advising on website design) and all aspects of studio production, including hands-on experience with audio editing techniques and all audio engineering duties. Including 5 years' experience managing all aspects of creative process management; creating the creative brief, selecting and hiring copy writers, casting, recruiting and scheduling talent, and ensuring the project is delivered in accordance with network directives and completed to meet all deadlines. Some of my work has been chosen for national TV and radio campaigns and I have also been seconded to third party companies on a short-term contract basis. Additionally I have helped in creating new promotional campaigns for both TV and radio for major clients like Disney, Pepsi, and KFC. Amongst other things I am responsible for a considerable increase in the picture/photo library, and I also helped upgrade our studio capabilities in LA. To this aim I created the configuration to eliminate studio and production flaws and also contributed ideas on the design of new studios. Things like label designs have greatly enhanced our professional presentation, and especially on the West coast.

Previous posts (1997–2012) include Board Operator and engineering assistant

EDUCATION
Miami University, 1994 Bachelor's Degree in Media Communications.

SKILLS
MS Excel
MS Word
MS Access
Pro Tools.
Adobe Audition
Cool Edit Pro
AudioVault

Lovely, but we've run out of space now, and I'm still hardly the shining star of the shortlist

INTERESTS
Baseball, swimming, running, movies

And now a bigger bubble for you to say a bit more about the CV in general:

I just feel a bit let down, I've plenty to say, but it's as if my best attributes have been ignored or hidden away — and for what?

COME IN CV NUMBER 2, RECEIVING ...

PETER R JAMES

22 Station Lane, Middlesbrough, North Yorks TS2 3YY
Tel: 01632 960411
Email: pjr80@pjr.com

PROFILE

Seasoned IT professional with diverse technical expertise and comprehensive experience in many IT areas including implementations of technologies, application of cutting-edge technologies, managing projects relating to technical, functional and operational guidelines. Abilities and experience include programming, coding, business analysis, consultancy, process optimisation, database design, standards, working with off-shore teams and delivering international project rollouts.

- Many years experience of ITIL/ITSM processes
- Experience in System Analysis, Design and Development in Axway Synchrony Gateway Interchange
- Advanced EDI, XML, IBM WTX knowledge
- Have used numerous adapters to send EDI documents across different platforms using diverse set of protocols, viz. FTP, SFTP, HTTP, HTTPS, AS2
- Experience in Interface development, Business processes, Mapping, Gap Analysis Technical Development. Functional analysis and Configuration
- EAI & EDI solutions, Design and Administration, multi-tier architecture
- Technical skills on IBM WebSphere Transformation Extender, IBM WebSphere MQ and EDI standards
- Configuration, Space management, Capacity Planning, and customisation of WTX in the AIX environment
- Internal and external 3rd party support experience internationally
- Domain expertise including Supply Chain Logistics and Warehouse Management
- ANSI X12, EDIFACT, GS1, OAGIS BOD, IDOC and bespoke formats
- Application maintenance, troubleshooting, production support and bug fixing experience

Is it just me or is all that mumbo jumbo?

SKILLS

- Protocols: SOAP, SSL/SSH, WebServices, FTP, SFTP, HTTP, AS/2, SMTP, TELNET
- RDBMS: Oracle 9i
- Integration: IBM Tivoli, IBM WebSphere Transformation Extender 8.2, IBM WebSphere DataStage TX 8.0 (aka. Mercator/Ascential), IBM WebSphere Message Broker, IBM WebSphere Message Queue, Oracle AQ, Axway Synchrony Gateway Interchange (Cyclone)
- EDI Standards: EDIFACT, ANSI X12, IDOCS, TRADACOM, RosettaNet, ebxml, OAGIS BODs
- Business Apps: OTM 5.7
- Languages: Java, J2EE, VB
- Web: CSS, XML, HTML, XHTML
- OS: Unix, Linux, Windows 9X/NT/2000/XP, AIX
- Project Mgt. MS Project

Admittedly I'm falling asleep here, but I could have sworn some of this is just repetition

EDUCATION

- Bachelor of Science in Computer Technology 1994–1997, York University
- Fundamentals, Map Designer, Database Interface Designer, Adapters (Database, HTTP, FTP), Event Server and Integration Flow Designer, FORTRAN, Pascal, Oracle

PROFESSIONAL EXPERIENCE

ABC UK Ltd   *Feb 2010 to date*

ABC is a leader in the world of IT services with 322 offices worldwide and an annual turnover of over £1 billion

IT Consultant
Responsible for providing IT solutions for SCi applications using OTM
Environment: IBM WebSphere MQ V6.2, OTM V5.6
Client: FG Global

Key Accomplishments:

- Implemented an Integration Gateway for the SCi application via IBM WebSphere MQ implementation with a flow of messages to and from the application.

- Responsible for preparing the Solution Design Specification documents and Business Requirements Specification.
- Worked with first/second/third line support to deliver WMS migration.
- Gap Analysis Report analysis of both Source and Destination, identifying mandatory fields and the business logics to be implemented.
- Drafted the Mapping Specification documents for business flows related to the integration and delivery of the new WMS system.
- Prepared Unit Test Plan & Unit Test Results Documentation and liaised with QA on both development and client testing environments.
- Assisted support with the resolution of assorted technical issues.
- Prepared the Business Requirement Specification Document and the Solution Design Document.
- Prepared the Mapping Specification documents for the business flows involved between the Management Systems, Integration Layer and SCi application.

XYZ PLC (formerly Cambridge Solutions UK Ltd)   *May 2004 to Feb 2010*

XYZ is an IT Solutions company to clients across multiple industries.

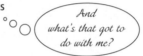

Analyst

Managed projects and technical aspects; this involved the design and delivery of requirements on system design, new technologies, performance/process optimisation. It also involved technology and platform analysis. Accountable for feasibility analysis, KPI's, risks, technical infrastructure, customer environment modelling, project evaluations, UAT and rollout.

Environment: Axway Synchrony Gateway Interchange, IBM WebSphere WTX V8.2, IBM WebSphere MQ V6.0

Client: FEG PLC

Key Accomplishments:

- Planning Requirement Analysis, Client Interaction, Design, Coding, Testing, Support and Documentation.
- Gathering and documenting User Requirements, Requirement Analysis, converting requirements into High Level Design Documents.

- Gap Analysis Report analysis of field attributes of both Source and Destination, identifying the mandatory fields and the business logics to be implemented.
- Message Interface Guidelines documentation for ANSI X12, EDIFACT, OAGIS BODs standards.
- Created Type Trees and Maps.
- Multi-part logic framework design and implementation.
- Business data exchange with client systems.
- Unit Test Planning & Unit Test Results Documentation.
- Hub Integration testing & QA.
- Review maps development and tuning.
- Deployment of the objects & configuration of the flows in the production environment.
- Mentoring Franchise analysts on Standards, Processes and Guidelines.
- Liaison with Franchise Analyst team/client and related solution providers to make sure project meets all specifications.
- 24/7 production support.

Can we just clarify – am I representing a person or machine here?

Other Programs/Platforms

♦ Mento MS Windows server 2003, SQL DB & Vmware ESX server, wireless networks, managed VLAN, Windows NT4/3.11 to Windows XP/2003 server environment, 3Ds Max scripting algorithms, Windows server administration using *Distributed Bucket Computing* algorithms, standards including *EDIFACT*, *ANSI X12* and *OAGIS BODs*, Pascal, C, C ++ language, FTP, SFTP, HTTP, HTTPS, AS2, AOD tools, object orientated design methods, Access and Excel

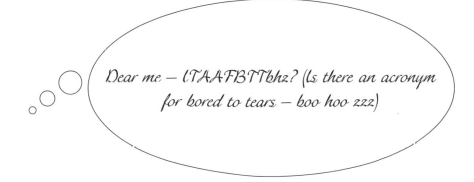

Dear me – ITAAFBTTbhz? (Is there an acronym for bored to tears – boo hoo zzz)

COME IN CV NUMBER 3, RECEIVING ...

Jane Weeks
76 Elm Grove, AB12 2NR
Jw122@gmail.com
07700 900432

- -

Personal Summary
I am a good listener
I am supportive of others
I have a good sense of humour
I am intelligent
I work well autonomously or in a team
I learn quickly
I have a 'can do' attitude
I share my knowledge to empower others
I am flexible
I am friendly
I am well read
I am funny
I am pragmatic
I am proactive and assertive
I am a good communicator
I am able to prioritise my work load to meet deadlines

Nice, but I feel a bit odd. Most of my friends have nice punchy profiles. I feel more like a shopping list

Education and Qualifications

Sep 2003–July 2006   Graduate of Aberdeen University (History)

Skills gained:
- Group work (including projects) and working independently
- Reports and working to deadlines
- Research of a variety of subjects

Hang on a cotton-picking minute. You're making me sound like a fresh new graduate – I've more to offer than that!

2001–July 2003 – Access to University Course, Aberdeen University

Employment History, Key Duties, Skills and Achievements

2006–Present: Administrator, ABC Ltd.

Fair enough, but is that all? I'm starting to feel a tad frail, neglected and undervalued

Duties:
- Assisting the managers and senior staff
- Secretarial and IT support
- Managing and overseeing office procedures
- Assisting with the recruitment
- Updating databases

Skills gained:
- Gaining more knowledge on administration procedures
- Building on my team working skills
- Enhancing my typing skills

Achievements:
- Successfully trained new staff
- Assisted at several meetings

Apr 2006 – 6 weeks work experience in a cake factory office.

2004–2006: Various temporary administrative positions during my studies including Receptionist at the Hilton Hotel, Aberdeen

97–Jul 03: Personal Assistant, SDF Ltd, Perth

Duties:
- Diary management and professional and personal support for the M.D.
- Scheduling to deadlines
- Booking international travel and schedules
- Coordinating database and Excel updates
- Recruiting cleaning staff

Skills gained:
- The ability to work to inflexible deadlines
- Multitasking
- Experience of managing junior staff members
- Attention to detail

Achievements:
- Project managing the purchasing and installation of 7 new PCs

95–97: Receptionist – HDS Ltd, Perth

Duties:
- Answering all incoming calls for staff and forwarding messages
- Managing front of house on a rota basis

Skills gained:
- Tact and diplomacy

94–95:   Telephonist – HDS Ltd, Perth

Duties:
- Answering incoming calls
- Booking meeting rooms

Skills gained:
- Developing a professional telephone manner

Office Skills
- Miscrosoft Word, Excel, Powerpoint and Outlook
- 65 WPM
- Photocopying, scanners and faxes

Hobbies
- Music, travelling, cinema
- Currently writing some short stories and poetry

References

Mr Jim Kelsey	Mr Jon Hume
Manager	Manager
ABC Ltd	DEF Ltd
Aberdeen AB1 2JK	Perth PH7 2UY

I'm sure you're a lovely lady, but deary me, I just feel like a timid little chick in a crowd of vultures.

Who's going to notice little old me?

9

Cover letters

I have made this [letter] longer, because I have not had the time to make it shorter. LETTRES PROVINCIALES (BLAISE PASCAL)

... the meaning of life, the origin of the universe, the offside rule, the secret to perfect chocolate soufflés and oh so many answers to literally thousands of wonderful, elusive and enigmatic posers.

... oh, sorry about that – my lovely but very professional editor says I have to stick to cover letters for the time being.

Hm, she may have a point, she usually does.

... ah well – another time ...

Cover story

It always surprises me when someone orders a professional CV but does not take the option of a professional cover letter to complement it. Most people do, but some don't, and in many such cases I strongly suspect that their job applications will be skewed, with a strong, high-impact CV accompanied by a run-of-the-mill cover letter.

After having read a great many DIY cover letters over the years, another observation is that a surprising number of people are not even sure what a cover letter is. Judging by some of the 'cover letters' I have seen, some people are evidently under the impression that a cover letter is a CV, or an essay, or a biography, or at the risk of upsetting a surprising number of readers, a sounding board to list each and every job and every last qualification.

As amazing as this may sound to some readers, a cover letter is none of the above; it is actually something conspicuously different – it is a cover letter. No more, no less. *So what is a cover letter? And what is its purpose?*

As the name suggests, it is essentially a letter, and traditionally cover letters were sent by post, just like any other letters. In today's high-tech world most cover letters are sent by email, and many people include the cover letter in the body of their email rather than attaching it separately. Even so, most cover letters still follow the same age-old format of contact details at the top, fairly standard salutations and opening lines, followed by some more detailed information about you, the job you are applying for, and what you can offer the employer.

If you examine some DIY cover letters you would be forgiven for thinking that their purpose is to recount the sender's life story in intricate detail. However, nothing could be further from the truth, and long-winded letters tend to completely defeat the object, which is to entice the employer to read your CV.

Consequently, a good cover letter specifically needs to be concise, pertinent and to the point. Yes, you need to let the employer know that your CV is definitely worth reading, and you do this by telling him or her the kind of things he or she wants to hear. However, if it takes you more than one page to do so then something is probably wrong, and in most cases it indicates that you are not writing powerfully, pertinently or concisely enough.

PRACTICAL HELP

Start your cover letter with your contact details. After all, if the employer wants to offer you the job, you want them to be able to contact you. Yes, you may have already mentioned contact details on your CV, but if they lose your CV they will have a back up means of contacting you. It is best to include your name, address, telephone number(s) and email address. For example:

Personal details

Jayne Marsh
156 York Avenue, Malton, North Yorks, UK
Tel: 01632 960333
Email: jm21@jm.com

If you are applying for a job with a reference number then include that reference number, e.g. Ref 23345, and always include the date.

If you know the name of the person you want to contact then add the person's name, e.g. FAO Mr Johnson.

It is customary to add the prospective employer's address to the cover letter, although most employers probably wouldn't even notice, let alone bat an eyelid, if you omitted it.

If you are applying speculatively start off the salutation 'Dear Sirs'. If you are applying for a particular job then either add the name of the person dealing with the application (if you have his or her name), or if you don't know this, use 'Dear Sirs'.

Most people mention where they saw the job advertised, e.g. 'With reference to your advertisement of 31 May in *The Guardian* ...' and I tend to do this myself, although it is far from a cast-iron requirement. If your cover letter is too long then this is one thing you could consider dropping (and especially if the alternative is omitting something which adds more weight, such as details of your qualifications, or relevant skills).

You should also draw attention to the fact that you have attached a CV and entice the addressee to read your CV, e.g. 'please find a copy of my CV attached for your attention'.

Then to the all-important body of your cover letter. After the introduction, the next part is the hardest: namely, telling the employer the kind of things that he or she wants to hear. As mentioned, ideally you need to do this in one page, and it isn't just a case of repeating what you say in the CV parrot-fashion or paraphrasing whole sections of your CV, you need to do it in a more original, pertinent and engaging way. This is the part that most people struggle with, and if you want the best results then it is an idea to engage a professional writer to do the job for you. You can get a quality cover letter from around £35, and frequently it is well worth the small investment.

But if you want to do it yourself then things to consider include how well qualified you are for the post, what experience you have, and just what you can do for the employer. If you can sell your key skills proactively and weave in relevant keywords in a concise and legible manner, then all the better. Obviously, it is a different format from a CV, so don't get sucked into the trap of *CV-fying* it. Yes, you should showcase your skills, and sell yourself in the best possible light, but at the same time try to keep things concise, simple and in perspective.

As well as considering what to include, you also need to think about what to exclude, because many people overcomplicate cover letters, and this is counterproductive.

The ending: if you are writing a targeted cover letter then you should sign off 'Yours sincerely'; if you are writing a speculative cover letter then you should sign off 'Yours faithfully'.

Remember that the most effective cover letters are *individual*, written from your own perspective and your own circumstances. Example cover letters are useful to some degree, but nothing is as good as a well-worded, pertinent and powerful original cover letter.

Afterword

To want to be what one can be is purpose in life.

CYNTHIA OZICK

Best CV

Many CV book authors try to convince people to buy their book by intimating that their easy-to-create perfect CV can guarantee you (or anyone) any job. I, on the other hand, said right from the outset that CV writing is far harder than most people realise. I also gave very obvious warnings right from the word go that you would never write an ideal CV by following the typical rigid advice.

At the same time, I also maintained that I did think there was such a thing as the best CV in the world, but *not in a form that you know it.*

If you have managed to read all the way to the end of this book without skim-reading, you will now probably have a far better idea of what I meant by this. You should do anyway, especially since part of the process involved thinking for yourself and listening to reason rather than rhetoric.

You could have a list of achievements as long as the Grand Canyon, or you could even copy Richard Branson's CV word for word, but it doesn't mean you would get your target job. In all likelihood it wouldn't. And why not? Well, for the many reasons and lessons we have learned in the preceding chapters such as relevance, writing with the employer in mind and optimising your CV to your own circumstances, needs and goals.

The best CV in the world for you is not generic, standard or static. It can't be copied from an example, bastardised from books, or compiled using special software. It is unique to you and is unique for you. It needs aforethought, planning, structure and meticulous execution. Significantly, the best CV for you isn't the same as the best CV for someone else. Yes, both would need to be sharp, pertinent, highly presentable and tell the employer what he or she wants to hear in clear, focused and powerful terms – all this and more. Even so, both CVs would still need to be 100 per cent individualised and completely different from each other. Not only that, but, pretty much by default, your best CV for one job will be different from your best CV for the next job – a right pain up the jacksie I know – and like other books, I could have just painted cosy rosy pictures for you. Indeed, it would have been much quicker and easier for me to do so – but at the end of the day I'd much rather you got the job!

Experience is a hard teacher because she gives the test first, the lesson afterwards. VERNON SANDERS LAW

Lessons learned

Rather than decree in dictatorial fashion that I had the magic formula to the one perfect CV, as many books do, I instead went out of my way to show that there is actually no such thing as a one-serves-all multi-purpose CV, and that many so-called CV rules are in fact just myths. I also demonstrated that there is a real danger in copying templates, examples and advice willy-nilly.

Hopefully the preceding chapters will have also opened your eyes to the immense importance your CV has to your career, and the fact that if you really do want to climb the career ladder then you need the best possible CV; a dynamic document which is original, specifically tailored for you, and optimised to sell you to the maximum for your target job. As we have learned, this is far from easy, but nonetheless, there are different ways to achieve this – and unlike what you are led to believe in some books, none of these ways are simplistic dot-to-dot style magic formulas. At the same time, options for success are open to each and every one of you.

Whichever of the effective, but alas less-than-magic methods presented in this book you choose, I wish you the very best of luck in your new adventures scaling your own personal career ladder.

Contact and further help

As mentioned, whenever I send CVs to clients I always ask for feedback, and I deliberately state that I welcome any comments (good or bad).

I wouldn't want to change the habit of a lifetime, so if you have any comments (good or bad) about this book then please feel free to email me at **paul@paulhichens.com**

I have clients knocking on my door from all corners of the globe, so I'm very busy and can't reply to each email, but the whole purpose of the book was to help people just like you, and if you think I have done that then I'd love to hear from you.

If there were things in this book you didn't like or you have suggestions for inclusion in the next edition then please just email me as I'd love to hear from you too (just not as much as all the people singing my praises!).

Lectures and CV master classes

I am also open to the possibility of giving more CV lectures and master classes. While lecture rooms and conference suites in deepest Dunbartonshire are perfectly fine, all expenses paid invitations to speak at ski retreats in the Alps or beach shacks in exotic locations may, for some strange reason, be given preference.

Next

I'm currently completing a radical new book to help you with a whole range of career issues from choosing the right job for you, to finding it, the application process, interviews and ultimately securing it. Please email me at **paul@paulhichens.com** to be notified once publication/ordering details are finalised.

Further help

If you would like specialist help with your own CV then my highly talented colleagues at **www.cvsucceed.co.uk** will be happy to help you. If you would like me personally to help you with your CV then I still write CVs, and details of my own personal CV writing services are available at **www.cvsucceed.co.uk/paul-services/**

Index